TOP-RATED
EVERGREEN
TREES

AND HOW TO USE THEM IN YOUR GARDEN

This book was produced for Western Publishing Company, Inc., by the staff of Horticultural Associates, Inc., in cooperation with Amfac® Garden Products.

Executive Producer: Richard Ray
Contributing Authors: John Ford, Robert L. Ticknor
Consultants: Claire Barrett, Fred Galle, Ralph Miller, Carl A. Totemeier, Richard Turner, Joseph A. Witt
Photography: Michael Landis
Art Director: Richard Baker
Book Design: Judith Hemmerich
Associate Editors: Michael MacCaskey, Lance Walheim
Research Editor: Randy Peterson
Copy Editors: Greg Boucher, Miriam Boucher
Production Editor: Kathleen Parker
Book Production: Lingke Moeis
Illustrations: Charles Hoeppner, Roy Jones
Typography: Linda Encinas
Additional Photography: William Aplin, Susan A. Roth
Cover Photo: Michael Landis
Acknowledgements: Jim Gibbons, Horticulturist, San Diego Wild Animal Park, Escondido, CA; Henry Koide, Presidio Garden Center, San Diego, CA; Bill Robinson, Japanese Garden Society of Oregon.

For Western Publishing Company, Inc.:
Editorial Director: Jonathan P. Latimer
Senior Editor: Susan A. Roth
Copy Editor: Karen Stray Nolting

Golden Press • New York

Western Publishing Company, Inc.

Racine, Wisconsin

Top-Rated Evergreen Trees

This book is intended to make it easy for you to select the best evergreen trees for a variety of landscape uses. The trees discussed in this book were selected by gardeners, growers, and horticulturists as being top-rated plants. They will perform outstandingly.

What is an evergreen? To many people, the term evergreen conjures up images of pines, firs, and junipers—the needled evergreens. But needled evergreens are only one kind of evergreen. The other is broad-leaved evergreens, plants with flat, leathery leaves. Both kinds provide year-round greenery.

Tree or shrub? It is sometimes difficult to categorize a plant as either a shrub or a tree, because differences aren't always clear-cut. Tall plants with a single stem or main trunk are generally considered to be trees. Lower woody plants with many stems are called shrubs. However, tall shrubs that can be used as trees are included in this book.

In the landscape: In most landscapes, trees serve as the dominant structural elements. They become the backdrop for shrubs and garden plants, and frame your home and property. Select and locate them with care because they become permanent and commanding features.

Plant names: Plants have many different common names but only one scientific name. The scientific, or botanical, name is used in this book. The guide on page 63 matches common names with scientific names.

Evergreens for your region: Plants are adapted to specific climates. The hardiness zones where each plant will grow well are given with each plant entry, and the charts on pages 5 to 7 provide further information.

At left: A group planting of pines *(Pinus sp.)* creates a forestlike home setting. Tree silhouettes add skyline drama.

American holly *(Ilex opaca)*

White pine *(Pinus strobus)*

Southern magnolia *(Magnolia sp.)*

Japanese privet *(Ligustrum japonicum)*

3

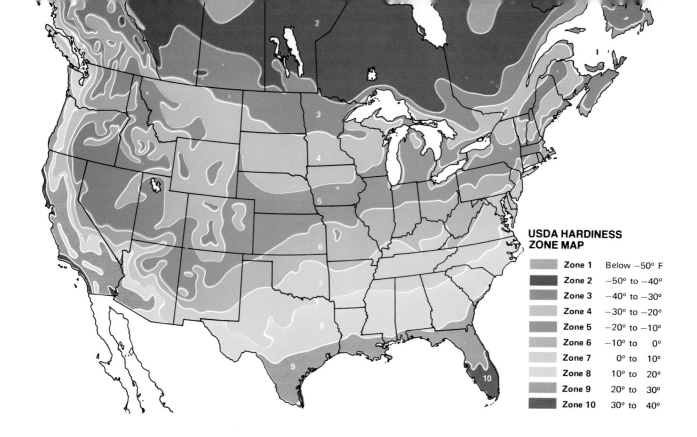

USDA HARDINESS ZONE MAP

Zone 1	Below −50° F
Zone 2	−50° to −40°
Zone 3	−40° to −30°
Zone 4	−30° to −20°
Zone 5	−20° to −10°
Zone 6	−10° to 0°
Zone 7	0° to 10°
Zone 8	10° to 20°
Zone 9	20° to 30°
Zone 10	30° to 40°

Climates for Evergreen Trees

The plant hardiness map shows the average low temperatures throughout the United States and Southern Canada. It divides North America into 10 zones with the average minimum temperature of each zone differing by 10 degrees fahrenheit. All plants in this book are identified in the following charts and in the encyclopedia by the zones where they are considered to be top-rated. Use the map to find your hardiness zone so you can select appropriate plants for your garden.

Broad-leaved evergreens are generally grown in areas with mild winters, although there are species that adapt to colder zones. Most needled evergreens are able to endure cold and occur in nature in all parts of the country, thriving in the North.

As every gardener learns, cold hardiness is only one factor of a plant's adaptation. A plant's ability to do well in a certain location depends on unique combinations of soil type, wind, rainfall, length and time of cold, humidity, summer temperatures, and temperatures in relation to humidity.

The USDA hardiness zone map does not take other climate factors into consideration. To give you additional information, the map and charts on the following pages break down the United States into 10 climate regions. For a plant to be adapted to your area, it should be recommended for your USDA hardiness zone and your climate region. For example, *Schinus molle* is recommended for USDA hardiness Zones 9 and 10, zones including portions of both western and southern United States. Climates in these two portions of Zones 9 and 10 are remarkably different. *Schinus molle* does well only in warm, dry areas of the West.

The climates around your home: Another aspect of climate important in selecting evergreen trees is microclimate. Microclimates are the small climates around your home that differ slightly from the general climate of your area. The northern side of your property, which is probably partially shaded most of the day by your house, is a cold microclimate. The southern side of your home, which unless shaded by trees receives hot sun almost all day, is a warm microclimate. A good way to become aware of microclimates is by making a site plan. (See page 12.)

Plants that are borderline hardy for your area may do well if you take protective measures such as providing wind or snow shelters and making use of your property's warm microclimates. Protected plants can often be grown successfully in the next colder zone.

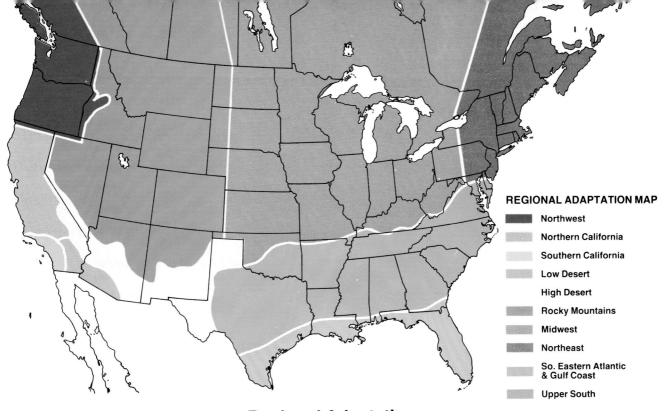

REGIONAL ADAPTATION MAP
- Northwest
- Northern California
- Southern California
- Low Desert
- High Desert
- Rocky Mountains
- Midwest
- Northeast
- So. Eastern Atlantic & Gulf Coast
- Upper South

Regional Adaptation

PLANT NAME	ZONES	NORTHWEST	NORTHERN CALIFORNIA	SOUTHERN CALIFORNIA	LOW DESERT	HIGH DESERT	ROCKY MOUNTAINS	MIDWEST	NORTHEAST	SO. EASTERN ATLANTIC & GULF COAST	UPPER SOUTH
Abies concolor	5-8	■	■	■			■	■	■		■
Abies nordmanniana	5-8	■	■	■			■	■	■		■
Arbutus menziesii	6-9	■	■								
Arbutus unedo	7-10	■	■	■	■					■	■
Cedrus atlantica	6-10	■	■	■	■	■				■	■
Cedrus deodara	7-10	■	■	■		■				■	■
Cedrus libani	7-10	■	■	■	■	■				■	■
Ceratonia siliqua	9-10		■	■						■	
Chamaecyparis lawsoniana	6-9	■	■					■	■		■
Chamaecyparis obtusa	5-9	■	■					■	■		■
Chamaecyparis pisifera	5-9	■	■					■	■		■
Cinnamomum camphora	9-10		■	■	■					■	
x Cupressocyparis leylandii	5-10	■	■	■	■	■		■	■	■	■
Cupressus arizonica	6-10	■	■	■	■	■				■	■
Cupressus macrocarpa	7-10		■	■							
Cupressus sempervirens	7-10	■	■	■	■	■				■	■
Eucalyptus sp.	7-10	■	■	■	■	■				■	
Feijoa sellowiana	8-10		■	■						■	■
Ficus benjamina	10			■	■					■	
Ficus elastica	9-10			■						■	
Ficus lyrata	10			■						■	
Ficus retusa	9-10		■	■						■	
Ficus rubiginosa	9-10			■						■	
Fraxinus uhdei	9-10		■	■	■						

Weeping fig trees *(Ficus benjamina)* have shiny leaves and a graceful form.

Regional Adaptation

PLANT NAME	ZONES	NORTHWEST	NORTHERN CALIFORNIA	SOUTHERN CALIFORNIA	LOW DESERT	HIGH DESERT	ROCKY MOUNTAINS	MIDWEST	NORTHEAST	SO. EASTERN ATLANTIC & GULF COAST	UPPER SOUTH
Hymenosporum flavum	9-10		■	■							
Ilex x altaclarensis 'Wilsonii'	6-10	■	■	■	■	■				■	■
Ilex aquifolium	6-9	■	■	■					■	■	■
Ilex opaca	6-9	■	■	■					■	■	■
Juniperus scopulorum	4-10	■	■	■	■	■	■	■	■		■
Juniperus virginiana	3-9	■	■	■	■		■	■	■		■
Laurus nobilis	8-10	■	■	■	■					■	■
Ligustrum japonicum	7-10	■	■	■	■	■			■	■	■
Ligustrum lucidum	8-9	■	■	■	■	■				■	■
Magnolia grandiflora	7-10	■	■	■		■			■	■	■
Magnolia virginiana	6-10	■	■					■	■	■	■
Olea europaea	9-10		■	■	■						
Picea abies	2-8	■	■				■	■	■		■
Picea glauca	2-5	■					■	■	■		
Picea omorika	5-8	■	■				■	■	■		■
Picea pungens	2-8	■	■				■	■	■		■
Pinus aristata	5-6	■	■			■	■				
Pinus bungeana	5-9	■	■		■	■	■	■	■		■
Pinus canariensis	9-10		■	■	■	■				■	
Pinus contorta	7-10	■	■						■	■	■
Pinus densiflora	5-9	■	■				■	■	■	■	■
Pinus halepensis	7-10	■	■	■		■			■	■	■

Leyland cypress *(x Cupressocyparis leylandii)* thrives in most regions and forms a dense screen quickly.

Regional Adaptation

PLANT NAME	ZONES	NORTHWEST	NORTHERN CALIFORNIA	SOUTHERN CALIFORNIA	LOW DESERT	HIGH DESERT	ROCKY MOUNTAINS	MIDWEST	NORTHEAST	SO. EASTERN ATLANTIC & GULF COAST	UPPER SOUTH
Pinus nigra	3-8	■	■	■	■	■	■	■	■		■
Pinus patula	9-10	■	■	■						■	
Pinus pinaster	7-10	■	■	■						■	■
Pinus pinea	7-10	■	■	■	■	■				■	■
Pinus strobus	2-8	■	■				■	■	■		■
Pinus sylvestris	3-8	■	■				■	■	■		■
Pinus thunbergiana	5-9	■	■	■	■	■	■	■	■	■	■
Podocarpus gracilior	9-10		■	■	■					■	
Podocarpus macrophyllus	8-10	■	■	■	■					■	■
Pseudotsuga menziesii	4-9	■					■	■	■		
Schinus molle	9-10		■	■	■						
Schinus terebinthifolius	9-10		■	■	■						
Sequoia sempervirens	7-10	■	■	■							
Sequoiadendron giganteum	6-10	■	■	■	■						
Taxus baccata	6-9	■	■	■				■	■		■
Taxus cuspidata	5-9	■	■	■				■	■		■
Thuja occidentalis	3-9	■	■	■				■	■		■
Thuja plicata	6-9	■	■					■	■		■
Tsuga canadensis	5-9	■	■					■	■		■
Tsuga caroliniana	5-7	■	■				■	■	■		■
Tsuga heterophylla	5-9	■	■				■	■	■		■
Xylosma congestum	8-10		■	■	■	■				■	■

Using Evergreen Trees in Your Garden

Trees are the tallest and most dominant plants in the landscape. Because of their size, they give structure to your yard and property, determining its scale and defining the boundaries of the skyline. Tall trees can shade your home and garden, protect it from strong winds, and provide privacy.

Evergreen trees remain green and essentially unchanging throughout the year, filling a basic need in every garden setting—a backdrop for the seasonal changes of deciduous, flowering trees and shrubs. Because they retain their foliage in winter, evergreens give the landscape a permanent structure around which other plants can be displayed. Both conifers (needle-leaved evergreens) and broad-leaved evergreens make admirable backdrop trees, though their effects are somewhat different.

Conifers: Conifers are characterized by wax-covered leaves that are shaped like needles or scales. Sometimes called needle-leaved or narrow-leaved evergreens, conifers are a diverse group of plants that vary greatly in climate adaptation. Some, such as the junipers, are extremely tough plants that withstand drought, low winter temperatures, and poor soils. Their needlelike leaves evaporate little water even during periods of high temperatures. Others, such as spruce and Oriental arborvitae, are native to cool, moist areas with rich soils and only look their best under similar conditions.

Conifers are fine-textured plants. Viewed from a distance, their needles create patterns of

At left: Variegated English holly (*Ilex aquifolium*) makes a striking specimen plant between home and garden.

Southern magnolia (*Magnolia sp.*)

Norway spruce (*Picea abies*)

Rocky mountain juniper (*Juniperus sp.*)

Leyland cypress (*x Cupressocyparis sp.*)

Common olive *(Olea europaea)* is a distinctive specimen tree for mild climates.

White pine *(Pinus strobus)* is hardy and fine-textured. Excellent as an accent tree.

thin lines that create a serene, calming mood. However, since most conifers are dark green and grow to a large size, they command attention in the landscape and have a strong visual impact.

Many conifers have a tall straight trunk surrounded by symmetrical whorls of branches. Their pyramidal shape is stark and commanding despite the fine texture of their foliage. Such formal-looking trees are best used as single specimen trees on large properties, and should be located where they can keep their majestic shape without needing to be pruned.

Conifers are common in the North where they play an important role in the landscape—providing green color during the long winter months. These evergreens, useful in creating a beautiful landscape throughout the year, also play a very practical role: They can be located to keep your home a bit warmer by slowing winter winds and preventing drifting snow.

Broad-leaved evergreens: These trees have flattened, often waxy or leathery leaves. They are flowering plants and many have showy flowers and fruit. Because they are evergreen, however, their year-round greenery is of primary importance in the landscape.

Broad-leaved evergreen trees are most common in areas with mild winters where wax-covered needles or deciduous habit are not critical for winter survival. Though conifers grow in the South and West, broad-leaved evergreens provide a greater diversity of form and function in these areas.

Because their foliage is often large and leathery and their framework consists of a stout trunk and a strong open framework of branches, broad-leaved evergreens create an entirely different landscape effect than do conifers. Some, such as magnolias, have a bold, busy appearance and so should not be overplanted. Others, such as eucalyptus, are fine-textured and are very effective planted in groups or groves. Contrast broad-leaved evergreens with fine-textured plants, or set them off against a subdued background such as a stucco or wood wall or an expanse of lawn.

LANDSCAPE USES

Evergreen trees have many uses. They are important ornamental trees as well as being problem-solvers in difficult landscape situations. The following are examples of how you can best use evergreen trees on your property.

Accent: Used to draw attention to a particular garden spot, an accent tree should be a focal point but not overpower the plants around it.

Background: Evergreens with branches reaching to ground level make an effective background for

Landscaping can camouflage the size and shape of a yard by transforming the dimensions visually. A long narrow lot appears wider if movement is directed toward the side property lines by a meandering garden path. Evergreen trees and shrubs are year-round structural elements of the landscape and should be positioned carefully to help create the specific garden effect you are trying to achieve.

Aerial view

Closely planted evergreen trees can block out unattractive views and direct the eye to pleasing scenery. They also form an interesting textural background for the seasonal splendor of flowering plants. A specimen evergreen tree located to shade the patio and house part of the day adds skyline interest, and might be selected to add the drama of spring blooms to the landscape.

Evergreen trees form the structural framework of the landscaping that surrounds a home. Select evergreen trees that are small in stature with colorful visual interest such as seasonal flowers or bright foliage to create a welcoming, shaded entry. Larger, more dominant evergreen trees define the property line, provide privacy, and are the richly textured visual setting for your home.

flower gardens and flowering shrubs and small trees. Fine-textured evergreens make the subtlest backgrounds, displaying other plants but not competing with them.

Color: Evergreens can be many shades of green: dark green, blue-green, yellow-green, and bright green. Some evergreens have brightly variegated foliage and others produce colorful flowers and fruit.

Entryway: Small evergreen trees are often used to highlight the front entrance of a house, creating a welcoming feeling.

Foundation: Small evergreen trees planted along the foundation of a house blend it into the landscape. Dwarf varieties are best.

Hedge: Evergreens make beautiful hedges year-round. Fine-textured plants are preferred. They can be pruned into neat shapes for a *formal*

hedge, or allowed to assume their natural shape for an *informal* hedge.

Screen: When privacy is important, evergreens, planted close enough together so their branches mingle, block unsightly views and give you privacy.

Shade: If properly located, tall evergreens can cast cooling shade on your house or patio. Be sure evergreens are situated so they do not block desirable sunlight in winter.

Shiny xylosma *(Xylosma congestum)* is adaptable and easy to grow.

Fir trees *(Abies sp.)* and cedars *(Cedrus sp.)* make an attractive pair and add skyline interest to the property line.

Colorado blue spruce *(Picea pungens 'Glauca')* is very hardy. Offers a regal silhouette and dramatic blue color.

Shelterbelt: Strategically located, a long row of tall evergreens with branches reaching to the ground will provide shelter from icy winter winds and hot, dusty summer winds.

Silhouette: Trees with beautiful outlines are a continual source of pleasure when placed so the open sky is their background. A tree's silhouette outlined against the sunset is a dramatic sight that can be enjoyed every day of the year.

Skyline: In open areas, a row or group of tall trees can create boundaries both on the ground and in the sky, making your property seem more intimate and inviting. Tall trees whose tops have the sky as a backdrop also frame a vista or far-off view.

Soften architectural lines: Small trees with horizontal branching patterns planted near the corners of a house blend it into the landscape and break up the lines of the house.

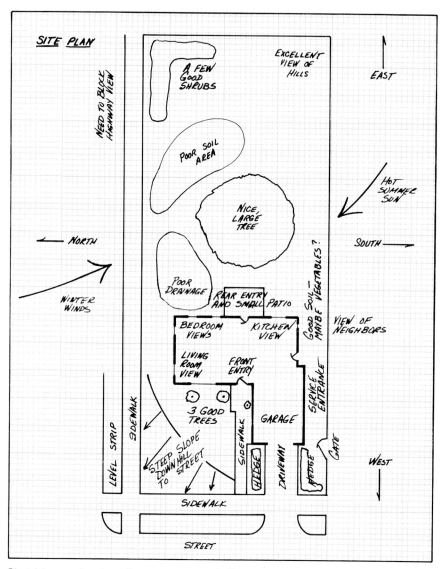

Sketching a site plan of your property, similar to the example shown above, helps you identify the landscape needs of your property. Once you note which views need to be blocked or preserved, where shade is needed, areas of poor soil or bad drainage, and paths of movement, you can begin to choose plants that meet your specific landscape requirements.

Evergreen trees have diverse forms to fill a wide range of landscape uses. As shown above left, group plantings of some species of trees create a woodland feeling and provide a sense of privacy and seclusion. Evergreen trees that bear seasonal flowers are a good choice for street plants, as shown on the right. Their bright show of blooms provides a welcome change from their all-year greenery. Evergreen trees used to mark a property line, as in the lower right illustration, serve as a windbreak and privacy screen and provide a pleasing bold silhouette against the skyline.

Specimen: A dramatic-looking evergreen makes an excellent specimen tree—one that is planted alone where other plants can't detract from its appearance.

Street tree: Evergreen trees used to line streets must be durable plants that can tolerate exhaust, possible road salt, and compacted soil. Their shape should not interfere with traffic, buildings, or pedestrians.

Topiary: Topiary is the art of pruning plants into fanciful animal or geometric shapes. Some evergreens lend themselves well to this treatment.

Windbreak: Several tall evergreens, or a line of them, planted in the path of the prevailing wind can slow down strong winds and protect your house and yard from extreme temperatures.

SITE PLAN

A site plan is a sketch or diagram, drawn to scale, of your house and yard. It shows the locations of doors, windows, and rooms, as well as trees, shrubs, garden beds, and outdoor areas such as patios and walks. Other physical characteristics of your property that might affect your gardening efforts should also be noted—good and bad views from indoors and out, directions of prevailing winds, slopes, sun patterns, and high and low spots.

Done properly, a site plan takes a good deal of time and observation. You should understand how the sun and wind patterns change with the seasons, since some areas of your property may be in full sun in winter but be shaded in summer. Noting the growing conditions of different areas of your yard will help you choose the trees and shrubs that will serve you best.

You can make an accurate site plan using graph paper and a copy of your survey. Record landscape features not noted on the survey, such as trees and garden plots, by carefully measuring their distances from the house. Mark trees and shrubs with circles indicating their branch spread at maturity. When you have a good diagram of your property, you can place tracing paper over it and experiment with possible planting and landscaping ideas before you ever touch a shovel to the ground.

Draw a circle for a new tree on the plan where you wish to plant it. Before making a final decision, check to see where it will cast shade and if it will have enough room when mature.

African fern pine *(Podocarpus gracilior)* grows slowly. Can be pruned as a hedge, espalier, or specimen tree.

American holly *(Ilex opaca)* is widely grown for screens and hedging. Unpruned, it makes a good accent tree.

CHOOSING THE RIGHT EVERGREEN

After you have made a plot plan or observed your property carefully, the next step is deciding which tree will do the best job in the locations where you need evergreens.

Besides trying to match the cultural needs of a particular evergreen to what the site has to offer, you should consider the visual impact the tree will have on the location. The look of a tree is determined by such things as its texture, color, and habit (shape). You will also want to choose a fast-growing tree if you want quick results and a low-maintenance tree if you haven't much time for gardening.

PLANT CHARACTERISTICS

Texture: Conifers generally have a fine texture and broad-leaved evergreens generally have a bold texture. Particular plants though, depending upon needle or leaf size and shape, will create a slightly different effect.

A plant's texture affects the appearance of your garden. Fine-textured plants seem smaller and farther away, thus making small areas seem larger and large areas even bigger. Bold-textured plants appear to be larger and closer than they really are. They can make distant areas seem nearer and open spaces seem cozier. However, if used incorrectly, bold-textured plants create a crowded feeling.

Color: Evergreens offer many shades of green and these should be considered when making your choice. Try to contrast blue-greens with bright greens, for example, so the trees stand apart from their background and each other. Also remember that many broad-leaved evergreens produce colorful flowers for several weeks of the year— the color of the blossoms should complement your house.

Habit: Some trees are tall and columnar, making a formal accent. Others are looser and more spreading with horizontal branches. If possible, look at the shape of a mature specimen, or look at the photographs in this book, before you plant a particular evergreen tree. Be sure its shape is suitable for your garden.

Growth rate: Many homeowners are impatient for their plants to mature and fill in the garden, but fast-growing trees often have weak wood or invasive roots, and may also be litter-producers.

Maintenance: Some trees require more pruning, watering, and spraying than others. Choose trees whose care requirements suit your life-style.

THE OUTDOOR ROOM

Visualizing your backyard or entryway as an outdoor room is often helpful in creating a comfortable outdoor living area. Think in three dimensions and use the same requirements you would for an indoor room. A patio, porch, deck, or lawn can be your floor. Hedges, shrubs, or fences serve as walls to provide enclosure, privacy, and a sense of security. A large tree or arbor blocks strong sunlight and is the roof. Specimen and accent plants fill blank corners. Paths allow easy access from one area to another. Barbecues and sink areas are included for the outdoor cook and there is a play area for the children. This approach may not be applicable in every yard but recreating what you like inside on the outside can make an outdoor area as livable as any indoor room.

SELECTION AID

The lists that follow will help you choose the right tree. They list trees that solve problems, have specific attractions, or fit into difficult climate conditions.

Use these lists as an introduction to the descriptions of evergreen trees in the plant description section. Do not decide on any tree until you have read its full description. If a tree is listed without a specific species, such as *Pinus sp.,* it means there are several species to choose from. Turn to the individual plant description before making a final choice.

The form and texture of plants, basically determined by the size and shape of leaves, growth habit, and color of flowers or other ornamental features, can greatly alter the appearance and apparent size of a yard. Coarse textures, bold forms, hot colors, as shown above left, make a garden seem smaller. Fine textures, delicate or simple forms, and cool colors, as illustrated above right, make the same space seem larger. By selecting appropriate plants you can create a feeling of open space or coziness in your garden.

Leyland cypress *(x Cupressocyparis leylandii)* grows rapidly and has a tall columnar form. Closely planted trees provide privacy and define property lines.

Pine (*Pinus sp.*)

Eastern red cedar (*Juniperus sp.*)

Privet (*Ligustrum sp.*)

Evergreen Tree Landscape Use Lists

Dwarf Forms

These trees are available in miniature forms ideal for bonsai, containers, or Japanese-style gardens.

		Zones
Chamaecyparis lawsoniana		
	Lawson Cypress	6-9
Ilex sp.	Holly	6-10
Picea abies	Norway Spruce	2-8
Picea glauca	White Spruce	2-5
Pinus thunbergiana		
	Japanese Black Pine	5-9
Taxus baccata	English Yew	6-9
Taxus cuspidata		
	Japanese Yew	5-9
Tsuga canadensis		
	Canadian Hemlock	5-9

Grown as Houseplants

These evergreen trees can be grown in containers in well-lit indoor areas.

Cedrus sp.	Cedar
Chamaecyparis sp.	False Cypress
Eucalyptus sp.	Eucalyptus
Ficus sp.	Fig
Laurus nobilis	Grecian Laurel
Ligustrum sp.	Privet
Podocarpus sp.	Yew Pine

Edible Fruit

These are dual-purpose evergreen trees, providing both beauty to the landscape and edible fruit.

		Zones
Arbutus unedo	Strawberry Tree	7-10
Feijoa sellowiana		
	Pineapple Guava	8-10
Olea europaea	Olive	9-10

Interesting Cones or Fruit

The cones or fruit of these trees may not be brightly colored but they are attention-getters. Many are also excellent in dried arrangements.

		Zones
Abies sp.	Fir	5-8
Cedrus sp.	Cedar	6-10
Cupressus sp.	Cypress	6-10
Eucalyptus sp.	Eucalyptus	7-10
Juniperus sp.	Juniper	3-10
Picea sp.	Spruce	2-8
Pinus sp.	Pine	3-10

Colorful Fruit

Brightly colored fruit can be a striking and long-lasting landscape attraction. Here are the evergreen trees with the brightest colored fruit or berries.

		Zones
Arbutus sp.	Arbutus	7-10
Ilex sp.	Holly	6-10
Ligustrum sp.	Privet	7-10
Magnolia grandiflora		
	Southern Magnolia	7-10
Schinus sp.	Pepper Tree	9-10
Taxus sp.	Yew	5-9

Attractive Flowers

These trees are known for their flowers as well as their evergreen foliage. They deserve a visible spot in the landscape. Those marked with an * have fragrant flowers.

		Zones
Arbutus sp.	Arbutus	6-10
Eucalyptus sp.	Eucalyptus	7-10
Feijoa sellowiana		
	Pineapple Guava	8-10
*Hymenosporum flavum**		
	Sweetshade	9-10
Laurus nobilis	Grecian Laurel	8-10
Ligustrum sp.	Privet	7-10
*Magnolia sp.**	Magnolia	6-10

Colorful Foliage

Colorful foliage can be as attractive as blossoms. Here are some evergreen trees that have colorful foliage or are available in variegated forms.

		Zones
Chamaecyparis sp.		
	False Cypress	5-9
x Cupressocyparis leylandii		
	Leyland Cypress	5-10
Eucalyptus sp.	Eucalyptus	7-10
Feijoa sellowiana		
	Pineapple Guava	8-10
Ilex aquifolium	English Holly	6-9
Picea pungens		
	Colorado Spruce	2-8
Taxus baccata	English Yew	6-9
Thuja sp.	Arborvitae	3-9

Japanese yew *(Taxus cuspidata)*

Indian laurel fig *(Ficus retusa nitida)*

Shiny xylosma *(Xylosma congestum)*

For Espalier

Here are the evergreen trees that lend themselves to the time-honored practice of espalier. Espaliers are plants trained in a flat, vertical plane. They are usually tied to a wall or trellis and branches are often trained in geometric patterns.

		Zones
Feijoa sellowiana		
	Pineapple Guava	8-10
Ficus benjamina	Weeping Fig	10
Ilex x altaclarensis 'Wilsonii'		
	Wilson Holly	6-10
Magnolia grandiflora		
	Southern Magnolia	7-10
Podocarpus sp.	Yew Pine	8-10
Taxus cuspidata		
	Japanese Yew	6-9
Xylosma congestum		
	Shiny Xylosma	8-10

Street and Avenue

These are evergreen trees commonly used to beautify streets. Tree habit will dictate whether they are suitable for narrow streets or wide avenues.

		Zones
Eucalyptus sp.	Eucalyptus	7-10
Ficus retusa	Indian Laurel Fig	9-10
Fraxinus uhdei	Evergreen Ash	9-10
Hymenosporum flavum		
	Sweetshade	9-10
Magnolia grandiflora		
	Southern Magnolia	7-10
Pinus canariensis		
	Canary Island Pine	9-10
Pinus pinea	Italian Stone Pine	7-10

Screens

When planted close together these trees form a dense screen without being clipped. Use them to block unpleasant views or to create privacy.

		Zones
Ceratonia siliqua	Carob	9-10
Chamaecyparis lawsoniana		
	Lawson Cypress	6-9
x Cupressocyparis leylandii		
	Leyland Cypress	5-10
Cupressus sp.	Cypress	6-10
Eucalyptus sp.	Eucalyptus	7-10
Feijoa sellowiana		
	Pineapple Guava	8-10
Ficus retusa nitida		
	Indian Laurel Fig	9-10
Ilex sp.	Holly	6-10
Juniperus sp.	Juniper	3-10
Laurus nobilis	Grecian Laurel	8-10
Ligustrum sp.	Privet	7-10
Picea sp.	Spruce	2-8
Pinus sp.	Pine	3-10
Podocarpus sp.	Yew Pine	8-10
Pseudotsuga menziesii		
	Douglas Fir	4-9
Sequoia sempervirens		
	Coast Redwood	7-10
Sequoiadendron giganteum		
	Giant Sequoia	6-10
Taxus sp.	Yew	5-9
Thuja sp.	Arborvitae	3-9
Tsuga sp.	Hemlock	5-9
Xylosma congestum		
	Shiny Xylosma	8-10

Clipped Hedges

These are trees that respond well to frequent shearing. Use them where a full-foliage, formal or informal hedge or screen is desired.

		Zones
Ceratonia siliqua	Carob	9-10
Chamaecyparis lawsoniana		
	Lawson Cypress	6-9
Cinnamomum camphora		
	Camphor Tree	9-10
Cupressus sp.	Cypress	6-10
Feijoa sellowiana		
	Pineapple Guava	8-10
Ilex sp.	Holly	6-10
Juniperus sp.	Juniper	3-10
Laurus nobilis	Grecian Laurel	8-10
Pinus thunbergiana		
	Japanese Black Pine	5-9
Podocarpus sp.	Yew Pine	8-10
Sequoia sempervirens		
	Coast Redwood	7-10
Taxus baccata	English Yew	6-9
Thuja occidentalis		
	American Arborvitae	3-9
Tsuga sp.	Hemlock	5-9
Xylosma congestum		
	Shiny Xylosma	8-10

Coast redwood *(Sequoia sempervirens)* Leyland cypress *(x Cupressocyparis sp.)* Carob *(Ceratonia siliqua)*

Interesting Bark

Shaggy, shiny, mottled, peeling, or brightly colored, unusual bark can be a valuable asset in the landscape. Visually, it lends a strong, rugged appearance, by adding structure and texture to the garden.

		Zones
Arbutus sp.	Arbutus	6-10
Cinnamomum camphora		
	Camphor Tree	9-10
Cupressus arizonica		
	Arizona Cypress	6-10
Eucalyptus sp.	Eucalyptus	7-10
Pinus bungeana		
	Lacebark Pine	5-9
Sequoia sempervirens		
	Coast Redwood	7-10
Taxus cuspidata		
	Japanese Yew	5-9

For Small Gardens and Patios

These are relatively small evergreen trees that fit neatly into areas of activity or limited space.

		Zones
Arbutus unedo		
	Strawberry Tree	7-10
Eucalyptus forrestiana		
	Fuchsia Eucalyptus	9-10
Ficus sp.	Fig	9-10
Hymenosporum flavum		
	Sweetshade	9-10
Ilex sp.	Holly	6-10
Laurus nobilis	Grecian Laurel	8-10
Magnolia grandiflora 'St. Mary'		
	Southern Magnolia	7-10
Podocarpus sp.	Yew Pine	8-10
Schinus terebinthifolius		
	Brazilian Pepper Tree	9-10
Xylosma congestum		
	Shiny Xylosma	8-10

Windbreaks

These are sturdy evergreen trees that can stand up to strong winds.

		Zones
Chamaecyparis lawsoniana		
	Lawson Cypress	6-9
x Cupressocyparis leylandii		
	Leyland Cypress	5-10
Cupressus arizonica		
	Arizona Cypress	6-10
Cupressus sempervirens		
	Italian Cypress	7-10
Eucalyptus sp.	Eucalyptus	7-10
Juniperus sp.	Juniper	3-10
Ligustrum sp.	Privet	7-10
Picea sp.	Spruce	2-8
Pinus halepensis	Aleppo Pine	7-10
Pinus nigra	Austrian Black Pine	3-8
Pinus pinaster	Cluster Pine	7-10
Pinus thunbergiana		
	Japanese Black Pine	5-9
Pseudotsuga menziesii		
	Douglas Fir	4-9
Sequoia sempervirens		
	Coast Redwood	7-10
Thuja plicata		
	Western Red Cedar	6-9

To Garden Under

These trees have well-behaved roots and cast light enough shade to allow other plants to grow beneath them.

		Zones
Arbutus unedo	Strawberry Tree	7-10
Ficus sp.	Fig	10
Fraxinus uhdei	Evergreen Ash	9-10
Ligustrum sp.	Privet	7-10
Pinus sp.	Pine	3-10
Podocarpus sp.	Yew Pine	8-10
Schinus terebinthifolius		
	Brazilian Pepper Tree	9-10
Xylosma congestum		
	Shiny Xylosma	8-10

Dramatic Character

All trees have their own identifying character. These trees stand out with a bold personality that catches the eye.

		Zones
Cedrus sp.	Cedar	6-10
Ceratonia siliqua	Carob	9-10
Eucalyptus sp.	Eucalyptus	7-10
Ficus lyrata	Fiddle-Leaf Fig	10
Ficus rubiginosa	Rusty Fig	9-10
Magnolia grandiflora		
	Southern Magnolia	7-10
Olea europaea	Olive	9-10
Pinus contorta	Shore Pine	7-10
Pinus pinea		
	Italian Stone Pine	7-10
Podocarpus sp.	Podocarpus	8-10
Sequoia sempervirens		
	Coast Redwood	7-10
Sequoiadendron giganteum		
	Giant Sequoia	6-10

Fast-Growing

These are trees you can rely on to give you a quick effect.

		Zones
Cedrus deodara		
	Deodar Cedar	7-10
x Cupressocyparis leylandii		
	Leyland Cypress	5-10
Cupressus arizonica		
	Arizona Cypress	6-10
Eucalyptus sp.	Eucalyptus	7-10
Fraxinus uhdei	Evergreen Ash	9-10
Ligustrum sp.	Privet	7-10
Pinus sp.	Pine	3-10
Schinus molle		
	California Pepper Tree	9-10
Sequoia sempervirens		
	Coast Redwood	7-10
Sequoiadendron giganteum		
	Giant Sequoia	6-10

Pine *(Pinus sp.)*

Common olive *(Olea europaea)*

Southern magnolia *(Magnolia sp.)*

Seashore Conditions

These are evergreen trees that can withstand tough coastal conditions. Those marked with an * are recommended for the western coast of the United States. Those unmarked are recommended for the eastern coast.

		Zones
*Arbutus unedo**		
	Strawberry Tree	7-10
Cedrus atlantica	Atlas Cedar	6-10
*Cupressus macrocarpa**		
	Monterey Cypress	7-10
*Eucalyptus sp.**	Eucalyptus	7-10
Ilex opaca	American Holly	6-9
Juniperus virginiana		
	Eastern Red Cedar	3-9
Picea sp.	Spruce	2-8
*Pinus contorta**	Shore Pine	7-10
*Pinus halepensis**	Aleppo Pine	7-10
Pinus nigra	Austrian Black Pine	3-8
*Pinus pinaster**	Cluster Pine	7-10
*Pinus pinea**	Italian Stone Pine	7-10
Pinus thunbergiana		
	Japanese Black Pine	5-9
Taxus sp.	Yew	5-9
Thuja sp.	Arborvitae	3-9

Heat-Resistant

These trees are star performers in hot climates. Use heat-resistant trees in the desert as well as in hot southern or western exposures around any home. Beware that many of these trees are not drought tolerant and may need regular watering during dry spells in order to survive the heat.

		Zones
Cedrus atlantica	Atlas Cedar	6-10
Ceratonia siliqua	Carob	9-10
Cinnamomum camphora		
	Camphor Tree	9-10
Cupressus arizonica		
	Arizona Cypress	6-10
Cupressus sempervirens		
	Italian Cypress	7-10
Eucalyptus sp.	Eucalyptus	7-10
Fraxinus uhdei	Evergreen Ash	9-10
Ilex x altaclarensis 'Wilsonii'		
	Wilson Holly	6-10
Juniperus sp.	Juniper	3-10
Ligustrum sp.	Privet	7-10
Olea europaea	Olive	9-10
Pinus halepensis	Aleppo Pine	7-10
Pinus thunbergiana		
	Japanese Black Pine	5-9
Xylosma congestum		
	Shiny Xylosma	8-10

Wet Soils

Soggy, wet soils with poor drainage are deadly for most trees. These are evergreen trees that are most reliable in wet soils. In areas with extremely poor drainage consider planting in raised beds or containers.

		Zones
Eucalyptus spathulata		
	Swamp Mallee	9-10
Ilex opaca	American Holly	6-9
Ligustrum sp.	Privet	7-10
Magnolia grandiflora		
	Southern Magnolia	7-10
Magnolia virginiana	Sweet Bay	6-10
Sequoia sempervirens		
	Coast Redwood	7-10
Thuja occidentalis		
	American Arborvitae	3-9

Drought-Resistant

Once established these trees remain attractive with relatively little water. Occasional watering will bring them to their prime.

		Zones
Arbutus sp.	Arbutus	6-10
Cedrus deodara	Deodar Cedar	7-10
Eucalyptus sp.	Eucalyptus	7-10
Juniperus sp.	Juniper	3-10
Ligustrum sp.	Privet	7-10
Olea europaea	Olive	9-10
Pinus canariensis		
	Canary Island Pine	9-10
Pinus halepensis	Aleppo Pine	7-10
Schinus sp.	Pepper Tree	9-10
Sequoiadendron giganteum		
	Giant Sequoia	6-10
Taxus sp.	Yew	5-9
Xylosma congestum		
	Shiny Xylosma	8-10

A Guide to Top-Rated Evergreen Trees

The broad-leaved and needled evergreen trees described in detail in this section were selected because of their top-rated growth performance and reliability in many areas of the United States. These trees are widely available in nurseries and garden centers in the climate zones where they are adapted.

Encyclopedia entries: Plant descriptions are arranged alphabetically by the botanical name of the plant genus, species, and cultivars, if any. For easy identification, the most widely used common names are shown in larger, heavy type just below the genus name.

Each entry includes the climate zones where the tree will give a top-rated performance and its potential height. The growth habit and other specific characteristics of the plant, such as color, size, and pattern of leaves or needles, bark color and texture, flowers, fruits, and berries, are discussed. Information on soil requirements, preferred planting sites, long-term care, and any problems is given for each evergreen tree. Facts about cultivars or hybrids of interest to the home gardener are also given.

Planning aids: To help you understand how to use evergreen trees most effectively around your home, the photographs accompanying the text and throughout the book illustrate the diversity of evergreen trees. Individual plant entries also discuss many ways the tree can be used to enhance the appearance, comfort, and value of your home and property.

At left: Deodar cedars *(Cedrus deodara)* grow quickly to statuesque heights. They are dramatic in the landscape as regal, fine-textured specimen trees.

Giant sequoia *(Sequoidendron sp.)*

Japanese black pine *(Pinus sp.)*

Shiny xylosma *(Xylosma congestum)*

Silver-dollar gum *(Eucalyptus sp.)*

White fir *(Abies concolor)* is widely grown as a specimen tree. Has fine blue-green color and symmetrical habit.

Strawberry tree *(Arbutus unedo)* makes a handsome accent plant. Fruits provide long-lasting color.

Abies
Fir

Firs are large, needled evergreen trees native to the cool, moist areas of the Northern Hemisphere. They generally grow at high elevations and are not suitable for sites exposed to strong winds, or areas with hot summers. Cylindrical cones are held upright on horizontally tiered branches.

Abies concolor
White Fir
Zones: 5-8. To 80-100 feet.

White fir is the most widely adapted fir. It is able to tolerate warm climates but is at its best in cool, moist areas. Needles are bluish green, 1 to 3 inches long. Needs ample room to develop fully, but can be grown in containers.

Abies nordmanniana
Nordmann Fir
Zones: 5-8. To 65-100 feet.

A very attractive evergreen with densely packed, 3/4- to 1-1/2-inch-long, deep green needles with silvery undersides. Can be grown in a container for several years as a living Christmas tree, but should have lots of room for development in open ground.

Arbutus
Arbutus

These small to large trees provide color throughout the year. White to pinkish urn-shaped flowers, orange to red fruit, and colorful bark plus shiny evergreen leaves make arbutus a top choice for specimen use.

Arbutus menziesii
Madrone
Zones: 6-9. To 20-80 feet.

Colorful, orange-brown smooth bark is the main attraction of this tree, native from British Columbia to California. Bark peels in thin sheets on small branches and trunk. When mature the trunk forms a dark, gray-brown bark. The tree forms a rounded, oval outline and grows at a slow to moderate rate. Glossy, dark green, broad, oval leaves, 3 to 6 inches long, last two years, then turn yellow, orange, or red before dropping in summer. Small urn-shaped flowers in terminal clusters, 3 to 9 inches tall and 6 inches wide, open in April or May. Orange or red fruits, 1/4 to 1/2 inch in diameter, are colorful from late summer into winter.

Madrone grows in sun or semishade. Soil should be acidic and well drained, but tree will tolerate drought and poor soils. May develop root rot if watered too frequently in the summer. Cool winter temperatures needed for normal growth.

Madrone is difficult to transplant, so should be moved when no more than 2 feet tall.

Arbutus unedo
Strawberry Tree
Zones: 7-10. To 10-35 feet.

Strawberry tree, native to the Mediterranean region, is more tolerant of a wide range of soils and climatic conditions than is the madrone. Natural growth is multistemmed and shrubby. With pruning, a small tree with one or more trunks can be grown. A rounded crown, as broad as tall, develops at a slow to moderate rate. Red-brown bark cracks to reveal smooth, red inner bark. Leaves are dark, glossy green, 2 to 3 inches long, with a narrow, oval shape. Small, urn-shaped flowers, white to pinkish, appear in fall and winter while the previous year's 3/4-inch fruits are still providing yellow to red color. Fruit is edible but mealy and bland, and attracts birds.

Strawberry tree will grow in sun or semishade. Soil can be acidic or alkaline, and either dry or heavily watered, as long as it is well drained. Will grow at the seashore, or in the desert if shaded. Needs some protection when planted in Zone 7.

Callistemon
Bottlebrush
Zones: 8-10. To 8-30 feet.

Bottlebrushes are known for their spectacular red flowers that bloom in spring and summer. However, they are evergreen plants and can serve a dual purpose in the landscape. You will find complete descriptions of the top-rated species in *Top-Rated Flowering Trees* and *Top-Rated Flowering Shrubs*, other books in this series.

Cedrus
Cedar

The true cedars are natives of mountainous areas of North Africa, Asia Minor and Asia. Best growth is made on well-drained, loamy soils in warm or mild climates. Young trees are conical or pyramidal. Needles are clustered on stout, lateral spurs. All cedars develop into excellent, large specimen trees if given ample space in which to grow. Not a tree for small gardens, although cedars can be kept dwarf if grown in containers. Upright cones on older trees are an added attraction.

Cedrus atlantica
Atlas Cedar
Zones: 6-10. To 60 feet and more.

Growing in the Atlas Mountains of Algeria and Morocco, atlas cedar is one of the few conifers native to Africa. Has the potential of growing to be 120 feet in height with a crown spread nearly as wide, but usually attains only half that size. Fast-growing when young, becoming very slow-growing as it reaches maturity. Old trees are flat-topped with horizontally spreading branches and are very picturesque, rugged, and imposing. Bluish-green needles are less than 1 inch long. Although slight shade is tolerated, best development is in full sunlight. Atlas cedar is one of the few conifers that can thrive on alkaline soils.

A number of cultivars have been selected. Blue atlas cedar, cultivar 'Glauca', differs from the species mainly in the silvery-blue color of the foliage. Weeping blue atlas cedar, cultivar 'Glauca Pendula', has blue needles and drooping branches. If not trained to grow upright, it will become prostrate. It is often used as an espalier. Heights from 15 to 35 feet, with crown spreads to 50 feet, may be reached.

Deodar cedar *(Cedrus deodara)* is a fast-growing conifer widely used in the landscape as a specimen tree.

Strawberry tree *(Arbutus unedo)*

23

Blue atlas cedar (*Cedrus atlantica* 'Glauca') needles have a silvery color. A statuesque tree to plant in open areas.

Carob trees (*Ceratonia siliqua*) cast heavy shade and tolerate adverse growing conditions.

Cedrus deodara
Deodar Cedar

Zones: 7-10. To 70-80 feet.

From the Himalayan mountains, deodar cedar is the most tender of the three species. Grows rapidly to 70 or 80 feet, with crown spreads of 40 to 50 feet, in 40 to 50 years. Lower branches are pendulous. Older trees are wide-spreading and flat-topped. This is the most widely planted true cedar in the United States. Requires well-drained soil, sunny location. Hardy cultivars are 'Kashmir' and 'Kingsville'. 'Aurea' has yellow leaves while 'Pendula' has long, drooping branches.

Cedrus libani
Cedar-of-Lebanon

Zones: 7-10. To 70-80 feet.

This cedar is conical when young but becomes flat-topped with age. Needles are usually bright green but varieties with yellow-green, blue-green, or silvery needles are also sold, as is a form with weeping branches.

Ceratonia siliqua
Carob, St. John's-Bread

Zones: 9-10. To 20-50 feet.

This species is a native to the eastern Mediterranean area. Called "St. John's-Bread" because the seeds and sweet pulp from the pods are supposed to be the "locusts and wild honey" St. John ate in the wilderness. Cultivated in its native area for the fruit pods, which are used for human and stock food. The pods, high in sugar content, are ground into a fine powder used as a substitute for chocolate.

Grows at a moderate rate, up to 20 feet in 10 years, forming a rounded shape. Plant width is usually equal to or greater than height. The bark is dark brown. The foliage is dense and composed of compound leaves 6 to 9 inches long with 4 to 10 glossy, dark green leathery leaflets, 1 to 3 inches long and 3/4 to 1-1/2 inches wide. If grown without pruning, a large, dense, rounded

shrub useful for screening or wind-breaks forms. Tolerates pruning and shearing and can be used as a clipped hedge.

Small red flowers form in short clusters in spring and are not showy. Trees are either male or female and flowers of the male trees have an unpleasant odor. Flattened, dark brown leathery pods ripen on the female trees in fall and may be a litter problem. Pods can be up to 12 inches long, but 6 to 8 inches is more usual.

Carob should be planted in a well-drained soil in full sun. Water infrequently but deeply, because root crown rot may be a problem if watered too frequently. Tolerates drought, polluted city air, poor and alkaline soils, and desert conditions. Young trees may need some winter protection but older trees are hardy to 18°F. Roots may crack paved surfaces. Carobs cast heavy shade.

Chamaecyparis
False Cypress

There are 6 species of evergreen trees, 3 from North America and 3 from Japan, in this genus. The species are large pyramidal or columnar trees. In their native habitat, all reach heights in excess of a hundred feet. In landscape situations half this height is usually reached. Numerous dwarf cultivars have also been selected. All require full sun, adequate moisture and good drainage for best growth. Sites exposed to drying winds should be avoided.

Leaves on juvenile plants are needlelike or awl-shaped, becoming scalelike in flat sprays on mature trees. The juvenile leaves are retained for varying periods of time depending upon the cultivar. Adult foliage strongly resembles some types of arborvitae. The Japanese species can withstand dryer atmospheric conditions; they are used in central and eastern United States. The western species thrive better where there is more moisture in the air.

Chamaecyparis lawsoniana
Lawson Cypress
Zones: 6-9. To 45-50 feet.

This species grows well on the West Coast. Mature trees have massive, buttressed trunks and short ascending branches, drooping at the tips. Care must be exercised when pruning. New shoots will not appear, as they will with other false cypress, if you cut into old wood. Seedlings are variable and scores of cultivars have been selected and named. These cultivars offer a great variety of forms, fitting false cypress into many landscape situations. Many excellent cultivars are available. 'Alumii', with blue-colored foliage, has compact growth to 45 or 50 feet tall and it makes a good specimen plant. 'Argentea Smith' is one of the hardiest. It can survive in Zone 5 on sheltered sites. 'Stewartii' has golden to yellow foliage and is also very hardy.

Chamaecyparis obtusa
Hinoki False Cypress
Zones: 5-9. To 50-75 feet.

Useful as a specimen tree, or in Japanese gardens. Many cultivars have been developed. Some of the better cultivars are usually planted in preference to the species.

'Gracilis' grows into a compact pyramid with somewhat irregular branches. It is slow-growing. 'Crippsii' has yellow-colored foliage, turning green as the plants become older. An extremely slow-growing cultivar frequently used is 'Nana Gracilis', one of the hardiest of the Hinoki cultivars. It is an excellent miniature tree for the rock garden or in situations where a large tree would be inappropriate.

Chamaecyparis pisifera
Sawara Cypress
Zones: 5-9. To 20-30 feet.

Some of the numerous horticultural varieties available are so different it is difficult to believe they all originated from the same species. Some plants have threadlike, long, slender twigs with few branchings, others have feathery foliage; some have long, slender needles that do

Dwarf Hinoki false cypress *(Chamecyparis obtusa* 'Nana Gracilis') is hardy and slow-growing. A good choice for small spaces.

False cypress *(Chamaecyparis sp.)*

False cypress (Chamaecyparis sp.) is a handsome specimen, lawn, or street tree.

Camphor tree (Cinnamomum camphora) can be pruned as a screen, or left unpruned for a shade or street tree.

not clasp the stem. Some forms are dwarf. Many of these dwarfs are slow-growing when young but accelerate growth after a few years, and end up being sizeable plants. Some change their foliage characteristics as they become older, while others retain their juvenile foliage.

The cultivar 'Filifera' has weeping threadlike foliage. A similar, golden-foliaged cultivar, 'Filifera Aurea', is often planted as a dwarf but will eventually reach 18 feet or more in height.

Cinnamomum camphora
(Camphora officinalis)

Camphor Tree

Zones: 9-10. To 20-50 feet.

Camphor tree, native to warm areas of China and Japan, is the source of camphor used in medicines. It is also a top-rated landscape plant. Grown without pruning, a shrubby small tree with branches to the ground develops, which is useful for screening or as a windbreak. With shearing, a formal hedge of almost any height can be maintained. When the lower limbs are removed, camphor tree is useful as a shade or street tree.

This dense, roundheaded tree grows at a slow to moderate rate, becoming wider than tall. The heavy trunk and thick, upward-spreading branches are covered with dark brown bark that looks black when wet. Small plates, like those of some oaks, develop in mature bark. In spring, pink, bronze, or reddish new leaves contrast beautifully with the leathery, yellow-green mature leaves. Leaves are pointed, oval-shaped, 2-1/2 to 5 inches long, and 1/2 inch wide. A strong camphor odor is apparent if the leaves are bruised. Old leaves drop in March and are slow to decompose. Greenish-yellow flower clusters, which emerge in May or June, are slightly fragrant but not showy. Inconspicuous, glossy black, globe-shaped, toxic fruits are 3/8 inch in diameter.

Camphor trees do not transplant well and are best planted from small containers. Planting sites should be in full sun and well drained. Camphor trees grow best in areas of high summer heat where temperatures do not fall below 20°F in winter. Trees do not grow well in heavy, extremely alkaline soil. Heavy but infrequent watering will encourage deep rooting.

Growing other plants beneath a camphor tree may be difficult because of very dense shade and the vigorous, competitive surface root system. Thinning out branches in fall may enable grass to grow beneath a camphor tree.

Citrus

Citrus

Zones: 9-10. To 10-30 feet.

Citrus are favorite small, flowering evergreen trees in the mild climates of the West and South, where they are grown for their fragrant white blossoms and colorful, edible fruits. They are evergreen plants, however, and can serve many purposes in the landscape. You will find complete descriptions of top-rated species in *Top-Rated Flowering Trees*, another book in this series.

x Cupressocyparis leylandii

Leyland Cypress

Zones: 5-10. To 90-100 feet.

This is a naturally occuring, intergeneric hybrid between Monterey cypress (*Cupressus macrocarpa*) and Alaska false cypress (*Chamaecyparis nootkatensis*).

Leyland cypress has a broad, columnar shape with compact, upright branches. The ultimate size is somewhat variable. Some selections have grown to be 90 to 100 feet tall. Others have reached 30 feet in ten years.

Leyland cypress is very adaptable and will grow on most soils with adequate drainage. Fast-growing, it will provide a tall screen in short order. Withstands heavy pruning, and can be developed into a hedge very rapidly. Set trees 3 to 5 feet apart for hedge plantings. Group plantings can also be effective.

Many cultivars have been selected and named. 'Leighton Green' is a narrow columnar form, strongly resembling its parent Alaska false cypress. Foliage is yellow-green. 'Castlewellan' is similar to Leyland cypress, but the color of the new foliage is a bright yellow. 'Silverdust' Leyland cypress is a cultivar with creamy-white variegated foliage. Tree growth is compact. Does not require as much clipping to form a hedge or screen as some of the other forms. 'Green Spire' develops into a very dense, narrow, columnar tree that frequently becomes multi-stemmed. Foliage is bright green.

Cupressus
Cypress

There are about 22 species of tall, aromatic evergreen trees and a few shrubs, most of which are subtropical, in this genus. Native in western United States to Mexico, and the Mediterranean region to China.

Cupressus arizonica
Arizona Cypress
Zones: 6-10. To 40-50 feet.

A native species originally growing in Arizona, New Mexico and northern Mexico, Arizona cypress is now grown from Virginia to Arkansas, and in the South and West. Young trees have a narrow, pyramidal crown. Foliage is light green. Bark on the trunk and larger branches is reddish brown, separating into long strips. Branches become horizontal as the tree reaches maturity.

Arizona cypress is fast growing and ideal for windbreaks and tall screens. It is useful as a specimen tree.

A number of varieties and cultivars exist but many are not generally available. The cultivar 'Gareei' has silvery blue-green foliage. 'Watersii' has a narrow compact crown. 'Pyramidalis' is compact and pyramidal.

Cupressus macrocarpa
Monterey Cypress
Zones: 7-10. To 40-60 feet.

Conical when young, Monterey cypress becomes broad-topped, losing lower branches with age. This picturesque tree was almost extinct

Arizona cypress *(Cupressus arizonica)* is fast growing. Makes an excellent screen, windbreak, or garden accent planting. Foliage shown below.

Monterey cypress (Cupressus macrocarpa) prefers coastal conditions. May be used as a windbreak or clipped hedge. Makes a good street tree.

The upright columnar form of Italian cypress (Cupressus sempervirens) looks stately and formal.

when discovered growing wild over 2 square miles on Monterey Peninsula, California, and the island of Guadalupe.

Withstands salt-laden air. Best cypress for seaside plantings where it develops a unique, windswept form. Use as a windbreak or clipped hedge. The cultivar 'Donard Gold' is a tight-branching form with golden branch tips. It should also be planted near the coast. Other cultivars with yellow leaves and shoots are 'Golden Pillar' and 'Lutea'.

Monterey cypress is subject to a destructive canker disease, and is being replaced by Leyland cypress, which is much hardier, in some landscape situations.

Cupressus sempervirens
Italian Cypress
Zones: 7-10. To 80-90 feet.

Native to southern Europe and western Asia, Italian cypress is commonly grown in California, the Southeast, and the Gulf States. Trees grown from seed can be quite variable in growth habit. Two general forms grown are an upright type with tight, upward-reaching branches, and one with horizontal, wide-spreading branches and a flat-topped shape when mature. Foliage is dark green, becoming so dark with maturity it appears black. Cones are among the largest of the true cypress, often growing to 1 to 1-1/2 inches in diameter.

Italian cypress grows best on dry, deep, sandy loams in sheltered sites. Upright forms can be used in formal gardens and along driveways. Trees will become quite large and are not adapted to small gardens. Pruning or shearing may be required to keep the trees symmetrical and dense.

A number of cultivars have been selected over the years. 'Glauca' is columnar with dense, bluish-green foliage. 'Stricta', a narrow, upright compact tree, is the form used in Italian gardens. 'Horizontalis' has horizontal branches, forming a wide head that becomes flat-topped with age.

Eucalyptus
Eucalyptus
Eucalyptus are vigorous-growing trees and shrubs native to Australia. They provide evergreen foliage, light shade, wind protection, attractive bark and flowers. Most eucalyptus are drought-tolerant but the growth rate of new plants will be increased with some irrigation. A mulch to keep down weeds and reduce evaporation will also increase growth of young trees. Good drainage is essential. Eucalyptus are free of insects. They were imported as seed and the insects that chew the leaves in Australia are not troublesome here. Also, they are not bothered by foliage disease.

Eucalyptus camaldulensis (E. rostrata)
Red Gum
Zones: 8-10. To 80-120 feet.

Trunk has attractive, dark gray peeling bark. Twig bark is reddish. Narrow, lanceolate leaves adorn weeping branches. Stands considerable heat and cold, and grows well on desert sites.

Eucalyptus cinerea
Silver-Dollar Tree
Zones: 8-10. To 20-50 feet.

A small species whose silver-blue foliage is excellent for cutting. The whitish bark and cream-colored flowers are very attractive.

Eucalyptus citriodora
Lemon-Scented Gum
Zones: 9-10. To 50-100 feet.

Lemon-scented, long, pointed leaves are the major attraction of this slender, fast-growing, high-branching tree. It has white to pinkish bark and white flowers that open in October.

Eucalyptus cornuta
Yate Tree
Zones: 9-10. To 30-60 feet.

A fine shade tree with a large head and spreading habit. Green-tinged yellow flowers form fuzzy 3-inch-wide clusters in summer. Adapts to a wide range of soil and climate conditions.

Eucalyptus ficifolia
Scarlet-Flowering Gum
Zones: 9-10. To 30-60 feet.

The winner among the eucalyptus for floral display is this medium-sized, roundheaded tree with leathery dark green leaves. Large clusters of light red flowers that are 1 to 1-1/2 inches across cover the tree in August. Large seed capsules develop after flowering.

Eucalyptus forrestiana
Fuchsia Eucalyptus
Zones: 9-10. To 12 feet.

This species has drooping red flower bases resembling fuchsia blossoms, which are borne intermittently year-round. Branches have a reddish appearance. Leaves are narrow and 1-1/2 to 2 inches long. Tolerates any soil and will grow in coastal or dry areas.

Eucalyptus gunnii
Cider Gum
Zones: 7-10. To 40-75 feet.

A cold-tolerant species that makes a good shade, windbreak, or screening tree. Small, blue-gray juvenile foliage is good for cutting. White flowers open in April.

Eucalyptus lehmannii
Bushy Yate
Zones: 8-10. To 20-30 feet.

Has short, blunt leaves of attractive light green color with tints of red. Small multistemmed shrub or tree. During July, huge clusters of bottle-green flowers appear.

Eucalyptus nicholii
Nichol's Willow-Leaved Peppermint
Zones: 9-10. To 40 feet.

A wonderfully graceful eucalyptus with a soft, willowy appearance. Leaves are light green with a purple tinge; they give off a peppermint scent when crushed.

Silver-dollar gums *(Eucalyptus polyanthemos),* shown above, are graceful shade trees. They have interesting rough-textured bark and bear small creamy flowers in spring. Varieties of eucalyptus offer a wide range of leaf shapes and colors. Nichol's willow-leaved peppermint *(Eucalyptus nicholii)* is shown below left. Fuchsia eucalyptus *(Eucalyptus forrestiana)* is shown below right.

Pink ironbark *(Eucalyptus sideroxylon)* bears pink flowers in spring. Bark is rough and attractive.

Pineapple guava *(Feijoa sellowiana)* bears edible fruit. Can be used as a hedge or screen, or pruned to tree form. Foliage shown below.

Eucalyptus polyanthemos
Silver-Dollar Gum
Zones: 8-10. To 20-60 feet.

A medium-sized tree, often multi-stemmed and low-branched. Oval grayish-blue leaves contrast with the rough, brown, or gray bark. Small creamy flowers open in March.

Eucalyptus rudis
Desert Gum
Zones: 8-10. To 30-50 feet.

This tree has rough, persistent gray bark, and broad or narrow, lanceolate leaves. A good eucalyptus for desert and coast conditions, but for best results, irrigate in arid regions.

Eucalyptus sideroxylon
Pink Ironbark
Zones: 9-10. To 20-80 feet.

Medium-sized tree with rough, dark red or black bark that doesn't shed like most eucalyptus. Lanceolate leaves. Masses of pink flowers during spring.

Eucalyptus spathulata
**Narrow-Leaved Gimlet,
Swamp Mallee**
Zones: 9-10. To 6-20 feet.

As its name indicates this tree tolerates poor soil drainage. Small, multitrunked habit. Red bark is smooth, flowers are cream with gold.

Eucalyptus torquata
Coral Gum
Zones: 9-10. To 15-25 feet.

This small eucalyptus is prized for its blossoms, compact size, and light green to golden-green leaves. Rough, flaky bark. Flowers are shaped like Japanese lanterns. Very graceful and attractive.

Eucalyptus viminalis
Manna Gum
Zones: 8-10. To 150 feet.

This fast-growing white-barked tree has an open habit with weeping branches. The willowlike pale green leaves and small white flowers from June to September are excellent features. Manna gum grows best in good soil, but will grow in poor soil.

Feijoa sellowiana
Pineapple Guava
Zones: 8-10. To 20-25 feet.

Considered the hardiest of subtropical fruit trees, pineapple guava is native from southern Brazil to Uraguay and parts of Argentina and Paraguay. Tolerating extensive pruning, it serves many landscape uses such as hedges, screens, or espaliers. By removing lower limbs, it can be developed into a small tree.

Growth habit without pruning is open and shrublike with many stems. Grows rapidly for a small tree, often reaching 6 to 8 feet tall in five years, with a width equal to the height. Pineapple guava can be pruned very heavily. Late spring is the best time.

Oval leaves are glossy green above and white-felted, with prominent veins, beneath. Size is 2 to 3 inches long and 1 inch wide. A variegated leaf form is sometimes sold. Spectacular, 1-inch-wide flowers have 4 thick edible petals that are white and slightly fuzzy on the outside and purplish on the inside. In the center is a large tuft of crimson stamens. Flowers are borne singly in the leaf axils in May or June. Fruit ripening takes 4-1/2 to 5 months in warm areas, 5 to 7 months in cool climates. Egg-shaped fruits are from 1 to 4 inches long, grayish-green, and often blushed with red. The soft inner pulp of the best forms tastes like pineapple. Seeds are very small. Fruit grown in coastal areas is more flavorful than that from hot inland areas. Fruit falls from the tree when mature. If picked too early, full flavor does not develop. Ripe fruit stores well in a cool, dry location. Can also be dried.

Growth is best in good loam soil. Will grow in clay soils but does not do as well in light sandy soils unless watered frequently. Drought-tolerant, though growth is better in all soils if irrigated. Grows best in areas without high humidity where temperatures are cool part of the year. Will grow in partial shade, but needs full sun for fruit production.

Seedlings usually fruit in 3 to 5

years. Grafted plants often set fruit in 2 years. Not all plants will set fruit without cross-pollination. More than one plant must be planted for fruit production unless the self-fruitful cultivars 'Coolidgei' and 'Pineapple Gem' are used. Plants are hardy to 12° to 15°F.

Ficus
Fig

This genus includes trees, shrubs, and vines, both deciduous and evergreen, many of which can be used for decorative purposes in the landscape and inside the home. All have milky sap and simple, alternate leaves. The edible fig, *Ficus carica*, is a deciduous representative of the genus. Evergreen species are frost-sensitive, but most can be grown in well-lighted, interior locations in cold winter areas.

Ficus benjamina
Weeping Chinese Banyan, Weeping Fig
Zone: 10. To 15-50 feet.

This broad-spreading tree of graceful irregular outline is native to India and nearby areas. Use as a patio or entry tree, as a houseplant, or prune to make an espalier or topiary specimen.

Normally branch tips weep and may hide the smooth grayish-tan bark. Thin, shiny, dark green wavy-edged leaves, up to 5 inches long, taper to a point. Light green new leaves contrast nicely with the dense, dark green older leaves. Small red fruits form in the leaf axils on some trees.

Weeping fig grows in sun or shade in frost-free areas and tolerates salt air if wind-sheltered. Leaf drop may occur with overwatering, or other environmental changes. Plants usually recover if the cause is corrected.

Ficus elastica
Rubber Plant
Zones: 9-10. To 15-40 feet.

This evergreen shrub or tree is used as a patio or specimen tree outside, and as a container plant outside and

Weeping fig *(Ficus benjamina)* is a graceful small tree used for street planting, at entries, and beside patios in mild climates.

Rubber plant *(Ficus elastica)* grows slowly into a round-headed tree. Young plants are useful in containers.

Rubber plant *(Ficus elastica)*

Shamel ash *(Fraxinus uhdei)* is fast-growing. Frequently used for street planting.

Sweetshade *(Hymenosporum flavum)* is graceful as an accent tree, bearing fragrant yellow flowers in summer.

inside. In its native India and Malaya it grows to 100 feet. A stiff upright tree usually grown with a single trunk. Large, thick, dark green oblong leaves can range in size from 4 to 12 inches long and 2 to 6 inches wide. The bark is smooth, brownish gray.

Ficus lyrata
Fiddle-Leaf Fig
Zone: 10. To 15-20 feet.

A dramatic contrast plant for frost-free areas. Also used for the same purpose in well-lighted, indoor locations. Outside, this tropical African plant can develop a 6-inch-diameter trunk on a 20-foot tree. Huge, fiddle-shaped leaves, up to 15 inches long and 10 inches wide, have a glossy surface and prominent, often whitish, veins. Increase branching by pinching.

Ficus retusa
Indian Laurel Fig
Zones: 9-10. To 25-30 feet.

Two forms of this species, native to India and Malaya, are used for street trees and as tub plants. *F. retusa* grows at a moderate rate, forming a dense rounded crown with long weeping branches. Closely spaced, 2- to 4-inch leaves with blunt tips are light rose to light yellow-green when new. They contrast nicely with the darker green older leaves. Small yellow to reddish fruits form in pairs in the leaf axils. Slim gray trunk is often hidden by drooping branches. *F. retusa nitida* has upright branches and crown. Can be sheared to formal shapes.

Ficus rubiginosa
Rusty Fig
Zones: 9-10. To 30-60 feet.

A native of Australia, this massive, broad-spreading shade tree grows as wide as tall. Heavy branches develop from single or multiple trunks. Bark is dull gray. Aerial roots, resembling those of the banyan, often form.

Thick, leathery oval leaves, 2-1/2 to 5 inches long and 1-1/2 to 2-1/2 inches wide, densely cover the rusty-haired young branches. Leaves are

deep green above and a woolly rust color below. Globular, 1/2-inch-wide, green to yellow fruits form at branch tips on mature plants.

Grows well in full sun or light shade in moist locations. Tolerates sandy beach soils and salt air, drought, and considerable heat, but not heavy frost.

Fraxinus uhdei
Shamel Ash, Evergreen Ash
Zones: 9-10. To 60-80 feet.

This fast-growing tree is used in hot areas of the Southwest and its native Mexico as a shade and street tree. One of the few evergreen ashes. In colder parts of Zone 9 most of the leaves may drop in January or February.

Shamel ash often grows to 25 to 30 feet in 10 years and 40 feet in 20 years. Erect and narrow with ascending branches when young, tree develops a roundheaded to fountain-shaped form with grayish-tan bark when older. Dark green compound leaves are 8 to 10 inches long with 5 to 9 leaflets. The 3- to 4-inch-long leaflets have toothed, wavy margins. Inconspicuous flowers in midspring are followed by conspicuous, large pendulous clusters of winged seeds in fall.

Three superior cultivars with very dense foliage are 'Majestic Beauty', 'Sexton', and 'Tomlinson'.

Hymenosporum flavum
Sweetshade
Zones: 9-10. To 20-40 feet.

This slender, open-growing small tree from Australia makes an excellent accent plant in sun or light shade. Shiny dark green leaves are 2 to 6 inches long and 1 to 2 inches wide. Golden-yellow flowers smell like orange blossoms and open April to September. Ideal planting sites are well-drained and not subject to coastal winds. Pinch young growth to prevent narrow, weak branch crotches.

Ilex
Holly

Hollies comprise a large group of over 300 evergreen and deciduous trees and shrubs native to all continents except Australia. They range in size from small, ground-hugging shrubs to large trees.

Hollies are extremely useful landscape plants valued for their glossy foliage, brightly colored berries, and adaptability to a wide range of growing conditions.

Most berries are red, but they also come in black, orange, yellow, and white. Male and female plants must be planted close together for the females to produce fruit.

Hollies can be grown in sun or shade and are best in slightly acid, well-drained soil. Holly foliage is usually thorned. Plants take heavy pruning. Tree forms are useful as hedges, screens, specimens, espaliers, and for background planting.

Ilex x altaclarensis 'Wilsonii'
Wilson Holly
Zones: 6-10. To 45 feet.

A hybrid between *I. aquifolium* and *I. perado*, Wilson holly is often seen as a small shrub, but can be grown as a tree. Large, attractive glossy green leaves are 4-1/2 inches long and 3 inches wide. Abundant bright red berries. Can be espaliered or used as a clipped hedge. An excellent choice for warm climates.

Ilex aquifolium
English Holly, Christmas Holly
Zones: 6-9. To 35-40 feet.

English holly is the traditional Christmas holly used in wreaths and holiday decorations. It is also a valuable slow-growing landscape plant, native to southern Europe.

Leaves are 1-1/2 to 3 inches long, and deep, glossy green. Some varieties are spineless. Others have variegated foliage. Abundant bright red berries on female plants.

Grow in partial shade in hot climates of the Southwest desert; elsewhere either sun or shade. English holly is sometimes bothered by leaf miner.

American holly *(Ilex opaca)* serves many garden purposes, making a good hedge, screen, accent, or specimen plant. Berries shown below.

Wilson holly *(Ilex x altaclarensis* 'Wilsonii')* withstands heavy pruning. Bears an abundance of red berries.

American holly *(Ilex opaca)* shades out hot sun year-round.

Many varieties are available. Some of the most familiar and reliably fruitful include: 'Angustifolia', which forms a narrow, cone-shaped tree with thin leaves and bright red berries; 'Balkans', a hardy form from eastern Europe; 'Sparkler' with an upright habit and shiny red berries; 'Teufel's Deluxe' with dark green leaves and large berries.

Variegated forms with silver-edged leaves include: 'Argenteo-marginata', 'Silver King', and 'Silver Queen'. Those with gold-edged foliage include: 'Aureo-marginata' and 'Gold King'.

Ilex opaca
American Holly
Zones: 6-9. To 50 feet.

Generally conical in shape, with spherical fruits that are usually red, but sometimes yellow or orange. Plant a male within 900 feet of a female plant to obtain berries. The leaves have marginal spines; the number of spines may vary. Leaves in the top of a tree often have fewer spines than leaves on lower branches. American holly resembles English holly, however its leaves are dull green rather than glossy. A few varieties have spineless leaves. Normally a slow-grower, although young trees may put on 18 inches of growth a year. A tree 50 feet tall could be 100 or more years old. Can be used as specimen plantings, screens, or tall hedges.

Native to southeastern United States, American holly grows up the East Coast to southern New England and inland through southern Pennsylvania to southeastern Ohio. In the Southeast this holly can grow on rather damp sites such as wet, flat woodlands. The farther away it is from the center of its optimum growing range, the more selective it becomes about site requirements. In the North good drainage and fertile soils are required. Best growth is made on moist, well-drained, slightly acid soil. Some cultivars of American holly are hardy in Zone 5 when grown on sites protected from wind.

Over a thousand cultivars of American holly have been named. Only a few are available commercially. 'Cumberland' and 'Carnival' are two hardy females for the North. Hardy males include 'Santa Claus' and 'Jersey Knight'. For the South 'Savannah' is a heavily-berried selection. Spineless cultivars are 'Kentucky Smoothleaf' and 'East Palatka'. Both are tender varieties. 'Morgan Gold' and 'Canary' have yellow berries.

Trees are shallow-rooted. Do not cultivate underneath the spread of the crown or you may damage roots. Use a mulch to keep down weeds. Leaf miner is often severe. Apply carefully timed insecticide in spring to control egg-laying gnats.

Juniperus
Juniper

The evergreen trees and shrubs of this genus produce two kinds of foliage. Young plants have juvenile leaves—sharp needles arranged in pairs or rings around the twigs—and mature plants produce adult foliage—scalelike leaves that hug the twigs. Some species may have both juvenile and adult foliage on mature trees.

Plants are usually either male or female. Females bear spherical berrylike fruits that may be blue or black when ripe. It may take 2 to 3 years for the berries to mature, depending on the species. Berries of some species add landscape interest.

Junipers may be heavily pruned or sheared for formal plantings. Tree types are useful as tall hedges, screens, windbreaks, or as specimen plants. If space is available, group plantings can also be effective. Most species grow poorly in shade and wet ground. Best grown on dry, sandy, or gravelly soils in full sun. Plants growing in heavy shade are subject to root rot. Essentially pest-resistant, junipers are hosts for cedar apple rust and should not be planted where apples are important.

Juniperus scopulorum
Rocky Mountain Juniper
Zones: 4-10. To 35-50 feet.

This species is narrow and conical when young, becoming rounded with age. Grows best on soils containing calcium carbonate, calcium, or lime. Best juniper for areas of heat and drought in the West. Many different forms have been selected because seedlings can be quite variable. The following cultivars are pyramidal to columnar and may grow to be 25 feet tall: 'Cupressifolia Erecta' has green foliage; 'Blue Heaven' has blue foliage and sets a heavy crop of berries; 'Gray Gleam' has silver foliage; and 'Moffetii' has blue-green foliage.

Juniperus virginiana
Eastern Red Cedar
Zones: 3-9. To 40-50 feet.

Native in 37 eastern states, this species can grow on a wide variety of sites, such as dry, rocky outcrops on slopes, flatland, and even on somewhat swampy land. Alkaline or acid soils can be home for this tree. This is one of the most successful conifers in Great Plains shelterbelt plantings because of its drought tolerance.

One of the oldest and most common cultivars is 'Canaertii'. It has a compact, pyramidal shape and is quite resistant to red spider mites. 'Skyrocket' is one of the most narrow and upright of all junipers. It is very cold hardy, with successful test plantings as far north as Manitoba, Canada.

Laurus nobilis
Grecian Laurel, Sweet Bay
Zones: 8-10. To 20-40 feet.

Grecian laurel has been cultivated since antiquity in its native Mediterranean region. Wreaths to crown Greek and Roman heroes were woven from its leaves. And its leaves are the bay leaves widely used as an herb for cooking. Many other trees known as laurels are so named because they have leaves of similar shape.

Eastern red cedar *(Juniperus virginiana)* is widely adapted; tolerates adverse conditions.

Rocky mountain juniper *(Juniperus scopulorum)* is hardy, tolerating heat and drought.

Grecian laurel *(Laurus nobilis)* makes a fine formal container tree, also good as a trimmed or untrimmed screen or hedge.

Japanese privet *(Ligustrum japonicum)* has fragrant white flowers. Takes pruning as hedge, screen, or foundation plant.

A slender, conical plant when young, it grows slowly into a broad, dense pyramid. A height of 15 to 20 feet in 20 years or 25 feet in 30 years is normal. Ascending but somewhat spreading branches will remain to the ground unless pruned.

Usually multistemmed, a single trunk can be developed by pruning. Smooth gray trunk bark is revealed when lower branches are removed. Stiff, dull green leaves are 2-1/2 to 4 inches long and 3/4 to 1-3/4 inches wide and have a distinctive aroma when crushed. Creamy-yellow to greenish-white flower clusters open March to April in leaf axils. They are not showy. Followed by 1/2-inch oval berries that turn from dark green to deep purple or black. Birds eat the berries.

Very adaptable, Grecian laurel can be grown as a small tree, or used as a clipped or unclipped screen or hedge. One of the best choices for a formally trimmed container plant and often used this way for an architectural accent.

'Angustifolia', the willow leaf bay, is a variety with long, narrow pale green leathery leaves having wavy edges. It is considered to be slightly more cold hardy; most Grecian laurels are damaged at 15°F.

Grows best in full sun, needing partial shade in hot climates. Grecian laurel will grow in most soils if they are well drained. Considerable abuse and neglect are tolerated without damage. It even grows well in city pollution.

Grecian laurel is subject to scale insects.

Ligustrum
Privet

This is a large genus of deciduous or evergreen shrubs or trees. Privets are one of the most common nursery plants, with some 20 species in cultivation. Easily propagated, privets grow rapidly, making them one of the most inexpensive plants to use as a hedge. In fact, the name privet is derived from its common use for hedges and privacy screens. They are tough plants that withstand heavy pruning or shearing.

White or cream flowers are born in terminal clusters in spring. Some are fragrant, others have a rather unpleasant aroma. Small black or dark blue berries are often quite conspicuous.

Grow privets in full sun or shade. They are not too choosey about soil and will tolerate city conditions. Will grow on rather dry sites, but best growth is made on moist, fertile soil. Most privets grow rapidly if fertilized regularly.

Ligustrum japonicum
Japanese Privet
Zones: 7-10. To 8-10 feet.

Large shrub or small tree commonly grown in warm climates as a hedge and foundation plant. Can be developed into a small tree, and is adaptable to topiary work. Dark green lustrous leaves and showy white fragrant flowers make the Japanese privet ideal for specimen planting. The variety *rotundifolium*, curly leaf privet, is a compact plant with smaller, rounded leaves. 'Variegatum' has leaves edged with white.

Ligustrum lucidum
Glossy Privet
Zones: 8-9. To 20-40 feet.

One of the larger privets, this species can be developed into a small roundheaded tree for use as a lawn or street tree. Large, feathery clusters of creamy-white flowers that bloom all summer make this a desirable specimen tree. Can be grown where root space is restricted; does well in large containers. Tolerates salty winds near the seashore.

Magnolia
Magnolia

This large genus has over 85 species of evergreen and deciduous trees and shrubs native to warm temperate and tropical regions in North America and Asia. Evergreen species are not hardy in the North. Valued for their large flowers, some species bear among the largest of tree flowers. Blooms may be up to a foot in diameter. Flowers are fragrant in many species and colors may be white, yellow, red, or purplish red.

Fruits are often quite conspicuous and shaped like cucumbers. Ripe seeds, attached to long silken threads, are released and hang for several days before falling to the ground. The leaves are large, coarse and stiff.

Most magnolias do best in fertile, well-drained loamy soils that hold ample moisture. Some thrive in peaty soils if they are well aerated. Mixing peat or compost in the backfill when planting is recommended. A compost mulch spread beneath the branches is beneficial when applied in spring and fall. Magnolias should not be transplanted after they become established, because injury to large roots can be very damaging.

Large-growing magnolias should be planted at least 40 feet from other trees or buildings to allow room for full plant development. Magnolias with large leaves are not suitable for windy sites, because winds can whip the leaves about, tearing and shredding them until they become unsightly.

Pruning must be done during the growing season, because dormant trees do not heal their wounds easily. If possible, confine pruning to young plants and small branches. Wounds made by removing large branches do not heal well and decay can set in.

Magnolia grandiflora
Southern Magnolia, Bull Bay
Zones: 7-10. To 80-100 feet.

Southern magnolia is native to the Coastal Plain from North Carolina to Florida to southeast Texas. Very fragrant white flowers appear throughout summer and fall and may be a foot in diameter when fully opened. Trees can grow to 100 feet tall with crown spreads of 30 to 50 feet. Shape varies according to site and variability of seedlings. Forest-grown trees can have trunks clear of branches for 40 feet, while open-grown trees may have their lower

Southern magnolia *(Magnolia grandiflora)* bears large white fragrant flowers. Needs ample growing room. Foliage shown below.

Magnolia *(Magnolia sp.)* may be trained and pruned to form a handsome espalier.

Southern magnolia *(Magnolia grandiflora)*

branches touching the ground. Forest-grown trees, 60 to 80 feet tall and 2 to 3 feet in diameter, are 80 to 120 years old.

Large leaves, 5 to 8 inches long, are thick, leathery and shiny green above, and a fuzzy rust color beneath. Foliage is dense and casts a heavy shadow. When grown from seed, 15 to 20 years are required for the tree to bear flowers. Grafted trees may begin blooming 2 to 3 years after planting in open soil.

Since this magnolia can grow into a large tree with a wide-spreading crown, it is not suitable for small gardens, but should be planted where there is enough space for potential development. Use as a specimen tree on the lawn, in the background, or in parks. To use as a street tree, set the tree far enough back from traffic so the soft, tender bark will not be injured. Some shade is acceptable when young, but full sunlight is required as the tree becomes older.

While southern magnolias are best adapted to Zones 7 to 10, hardy strains are continually being developed and tested, with the hope of extending the planting of this tree farther north. Some hardy strains have survived into Zone 6 on protected sites. Leaves will often be killed at temperatures of 10° to 15°F. Some cultivars with special characteristics include: 'Russet' with small leaves and dense foliage on compact branches; 'Samuel Sommer' with extremely fragrant flowers up to 14 inches in diameter and leaves 10 inches or more in length; and 'St. Mary', a smaller form, which grows to 20 feet, making it ideal for small garden or street use. It has an especially heavy bloom.

Magnolia virginiana
Sweet Bay Magnolia
Zones: 6-10. To 60 feet.

Trees of this species will reach 60 feet tall in southern United States. In other areas, and even sometimes in the South, it forms a shrub 10 to 20 feet tall with a crown spread of 10 to 20 feet. Native from coastal Massachusettes to Florida, west to

Tennessee and Texas, some varieties will grow in Zone 5 on sheltered sites.

Sweet bay magnolia will grow in quite swampy areas and on moist, but well-drained sites. Evergreen to semievergreen in the South and deciduous in the North. Prefers acid soil with pH of 5.0 to 6.5.

Plant as a small patio tree, a specimen plant, or in foundation plantings. In the extreme northern part of its growing area it should be set in protected locations, such as the north side of a building where winter sunshine will not harm the foliage.

Sweet bay magnolia has a tendency to be multistemmed, and pruning and training will usually be required to develop a single-stemmed tree.

White or creamy-white globular flowers are 2 to 3 inches wide. They are fragrant and do not all bloom at once. Bloom is extended over several weeks.

Olea europaea
Common Olive
Zones: 9-10. To 25-30 feet.

Cultivated in the eastern Mediterranean area since ancient times, fruiting trees over 1,000 years old are known. Trees planted in California by the Spanish missionaries in the 1700's are still producing. Besides being grown for fruit, olives make striking, gray-green-foliaged street and landscape trees.

A dense, rounded tree develops in poor soil with little water. Under better conditions, growth is irregular and more open. In both situations height and width are similar, but young trees with good growing conditions develop height quickly, then fill out slowly. Low branching is normal. Most trees are multi-trunked.

Bark is smooth and gray when young, becoming rough and dark brown on old trees. Willowlike leaves, 1-1 2 to 3 inches long, are gray-green on the upper surface and silver beneath. Fragrant, tiny, yellow-white, wind-pollinated flowers appear on two-year-old branches during April and May. Glossy fruits, 1/2 to 1-1/2 inches long, ripen in fall after changing from green to purple and finally to black and wrinkled. They are inedible without special processing.

Three varieties are most commonly planted in the landscape. 'Fruitless', used only for landscaping, sometimes does have fruit. 'Manzanillo' is a low-growing, spreading, large-fruited variety used both commercially and for landscaping. 'Mission' is taller, more compact, hardier and used for both purposes.

Olives are hardy to 15°F. They should be planted in full sun and well-drained soil. Faster growth occurs on moist, fertile soil but a more attractive, contorted shape develops on poor, dry, shallow, or alkaline soils. Grows well in hot, dry conditions as well as cool, moist coastal regions of California. Fruiting is not reliable in warm, humid areas of the southern United States.

Fruit stains any surface on which it falls. Nonfruiting varieties, picking, or hormone sprays can be used to reduce fruit set.

Picea
Spruce

Picea is one of the largest and most important genera of conifers. Spruces are mostly large conical trees growing in the cool, temperate regions of the Northern Hemisphere. In the southern United States growing areas are confined to high elevations. Spruces grow on most kinds of soil, providing there is good drainage and ample moisture. *P. omorika* and *P. pungens* are more tolerant of dry or poor soils than other species.

Trees are single-stemmed. Most spruce are shallow-rooted and suffer during droughts unless watered.

Needles are retained 6 to 8 years, unless affected by drought, making a dense foliage. Cones are pendulous, adding interest to the trees. Most species mature at 100 feet or more. Not for small properties, unless you plan on removing them when they outgrow allotted space.

Common olive *(Olea europaea)* has gray-green leaves and an interesting contorted trunk, making a specimen tree with rugged character.

Alberta spruce *(Picea glauca albertiana)* has a very dense, fine-textured foliage. Makes a unique accent plant.

Norway spruce *(Picea abies)*

If planted in front of your house, they will eventually hide it. You can also select one of the slow-growing or dwarf varieties. Use as windbreaks, shelterbelts, in group plantings, or background plantings on large properties.

Prune as needed in early spring, to nip back a branch that is destroying the symmetrical shape or to remove a double top. Most spruces are damaged by deicing salt and should not be planted where run-off or drifting spray caused by traffic could be a problem.

Picea abies
Norway Spruce
Zones: 2-8. To 90-100 feet.

Young Norway spruce tend to be conical in shape with upright branches covered with short, shiny dark green needles. As trees become older, side branches become more horizontal and frequently pendulous branchlets develop. When trees reach 30 years, crowns begin to become more open, giving a picturesque appearance. Branches appear stiff when young but become more graceful at maturity.

Cones, among the largest of all spruces, are 6 or more inches long.

Norway spruce is the most widely grown spruce in cultivation, and has been grown as an ornamental tree in Europe for over 500 years.

This thirsty tree requires abundant moisture, especially when young. Growth is fast for a spruce, with height increases of a foot or more a year. Most Norway spruce are grown from seed so variations in form occur. Selected cultivars include 'Pendula' with drooping branches and 'Pyramidata', a slender form.

Picea glauca
White Spruce
Zones: 2-5. To 70-80 feet.

This north country tree grows from Alaska to Labrador and northeast United States. In Canada it grows into the permafrost zone. White spruce is recommended especially for the northern Midwest where it can endure the severe heat and cold. Elsewhere, other spruces are more attractive alternatives.

Slow-growing varieties suitable for smaller properties are often planted. Black Hills spruce, 'Densata', has very dense bluish-green foliage. Alberta spruce, variety *albertiana*, is a narrow, compact tree.

Picea omorika
Serbian Spruce
Zones: 5-8. To 75-100 feet.

One of the most graceful of all spruces. Typically a narrow cone shape, occupying less space than most spruces. Branches are short and drooping, curving upward at the tips. The glossy green needles have silver undersides. One of the toughest of the spruce, this species should be more widely planted.

Picea pungens
Colorado Spruce
Zones: 2-8. To 75-100 feet.

A formal-looking tree. Colorado spruce is symmetrical with whorls of stiff branches. Needles are sharp and vary in color from green to blue.

This tree is often called blue spruce. The group 'Glauca' includes blue forms which usually are propagated by grafting. The blue color is due to a wax or powder covering the needles. Blueness on older trees can weather away and needles turn green. Some pesticide sprays can also remove the blue color.

Many cultivars have been selected from especially desirable trees. 'Moerheimii', a blue selection, has been available since 1912. The foliage is quite dense with branches forming a layered or tiered effect. Fifty-year-old trees are 30 feet tall. 'Koster', also with blue foliage and a more compact form, has been around since 1885. The bluest of all varieties is 'Hoopsii'.

Colorado blue spruce *(Picea pungens 'Glauca')* grows at a moderate rate, retaining its symmetrical shape.

Pinus
Pine

This large genus contains 90 species of usually tall coniferous trees. A few species are naturally dwarf and compact, and many shrubby and dwarf cultivars have been selected from other species.

Pines are native to the Northern Hemisphere with different species growing from the cold northern latitudes to the tropics. Many species are planted as ornamentals. Most are best suited to large areas as a single specimen or silhouette tree; some make useful windbreaks and shelterbelts. Leaves are needlelike, usually borne in clusters of 2 to 5, rarely 1.

Pinus aristata
Bristlecone Pine
Zones: 5-6. To 12-15 feet.

There is a stand of bristlecone pines in the Sierra Nevadas that is 5,000 years old; these trees are considered to be the oldest living things. Bristlecone pines are very slow-growing, possibly reaching 15 feet in 65 years. Form is irregular and twisted. Needles are held 20 to 30 years, giving a brushy appearance to branch ends. Needles, in 5's, are 1 to 1-1/2 inches long and flecked with pitchy dots. Use in small gardens.

Pinus bungeana
Lacebark Pine
Zones: 5-9. To 80 feet.

This multistemmed, pyramidal to round-topped tree has handsome bark mottled gray-green and creamy. Bright green needles are 3 inches long. Slow-growing. Do not plant in areas subject to drift or run-off of deicing salts.

Pinus canariensis
Canary Island Pine
Zones: 9-10. To 90 feet.

Young trees are fast-growing and pyramidal. Older trees have broad rounded crowns. Needles are long and weeping. Good as a shade tree because lower branches do not persist. A tree for California and the extreme South. Drought-resistant.

White pine *(Pinus strobus)* is widely planted as a graceful specimen tree. Also makes a beautiful screen. Needle cluster with growth candle shown below.

Canary island pine (Pinus canariensis) loses lower branches and makes a stately lawn or street tree.

Japanese black pine (Pinus thunbergiana) is fast growing and tolerates adverse conditions.

Pinus contorta
Shore Pine
Zones: 7-10. To 30 feet.

A fast-growing tree, with somewhat irregular crown, suitable for small gardens. Dark green needles are 1-1/4 to 2 inches long. Grows well on light sandy coastal soils, dislikes lime. Will grow on boggy and dry soils, but not on hot, dry sites.

Pinus densiflora
Japanese Red Pine
Zones: 5-9. To 90-100 feet.

Has a conical shape when young, becomes irregular and flat-topped with age. Orange-red scaling bark adds interest. Slender, bright blue-green or yellow-green needles are 2-1/2 to 5 inches long. Picturesque tree for informal gardens.

Pinus halepensis
Aleppo Pine
Zones: 7-10. To 30-50 feet.

This rounded, open-crown tree sometimes appears shrubby. Light green needles are 2-1/2 to 4 inches long. Suitable for hot, dry areas, such as seaside and desert regions. Much planted in Mediterranean region and excellent for California. The variety *eldarica* grows taller with a pyramidal crown. Noted for fast growth and ability to stand heat.

Pinus nigra
Austrian Black Pine
Zones: 3-8. To 60-120 feet.

Conical when young, this tree loses bottom branches and becomes umbrella-shaped when mature. Sharp, stiff very dark green needles are 3 to 6-1/2 inches long. Will grow on acid or limestone soils, withstands extreme conditions, and is tolerant of drift from deicing salts.

Pinus patula
Jelecote Pine
Zones: 9-10. To 40-80 feet.

Very fast-growing with loose, open pyramidal crown made up of layers of tiered branches. Needles to 9 inches long. A silhouette tree, best adapted to southern, coastal California. Can also be grown in more northern regions of coastal Pacific Northwest. Casts a light shadow.

Pinus pinaster
Cluster Pine, French Turpentine Pine, Maritime Pine
Zones: 7-10. To 60-90 feet.

Cluster pine forms a conical crown with spreading branches. Glossy green, stiff needles are 5 to 9 inches long. Thrives on well-drained, sandy soils. Dislikes clay soils. Well adapted to seaside planting. Used to stabilize sand dunes.

Pinus pinea
Italian Stone Pine
Zones: 7-10. To 30-75 feet.

Trees are globular and bushy when young, becoming flat-topped, umbrella-shaped, and distinctive at maturity. Stiff, bright to gray-green needles are 5 to 8 inches long. Large, edible seeds. Hardy, withstanding heat and drought once established. Grows in California and the Pacific Northwest, and does well in coastal areas.

Pinus strobus
White Pine
Zones: 2-8. To 100-150 feet.

This beautiful pine is widely planted in the Eastern United States, where it can be very long-lived. Needles are blue-green, 3 to 5 inches long, and soft-textured. Trees are graceful and open-branched. 'Fastigiata' is a narrow, columnar form. 'Pendula' is a decorative, weeping form.

White pines are best grown on well-drained sites out of the wind. A serious fungus disease, white pine blister rust, infects these pines. The rust is carried by currant and gooseberry bushes; plant pines at least 900 feet away from these host plants.

Pinus sylvestris
Scotch Pine
Zones: 3-8. To 70-100 feet.

Can be quite variable in shape depending upon seed source. Attractive orange-red bark. Blue-green needles are stiff, 1-1/2 to 3 inches long. Grow as windbreaks, specimen trees, for shade, and as Christmas trees. Must be grown in full sunlight. Not for desert areas. Damaged by spray from deicing salts.

Pinus thunbergiana
Japanese Black Pine.
Zones: 5-9. To 60-90 feet.

Broad pyramidal crown becomes irregular at maturity. Fast-growing, with 3- to 4-1/2-inch-long, bright green, stiff needles. Best growth on moist, fertile, well-drained soils, but will grow on sandy soils. Can be used for stabilizing sand dunes. Proven to be one of the best pines for seaside plantings in northeastern United States. Grows under adverse conditions and tolerates spray from deicing salts. Set in full sunlight for best development. Adaptable to pruning. Can be trained to a variety of forms. The Japanese use it in bonsai and have developed many different types. 'Oculus-draconis' has needles striped with 2 yellow bands.

Podocarpus
Yew Pine

Native to the Southern Hemisphere and the Orient. Closely related to yew, *Taxus sp.*, yew pines also have a fleshy, berrylike fruit. They are used as street and lawn trees, and for many of the same purposes as yews: clipped hedges, topiaries, tub plants, and specimen plants. Often planted as shrubs in mild climate gardens, where they later grow into trees.

Podocarpus gracilior
African Fern Pine
Zones: 9-10. To 50-60 feet.

This is a slow-growing native of East Africa. Variable habit and form depend on the age and propagation method. Plants grown by cuttings from mature trees are limber and slow to develop upright stems; they have gray or blue-green leaves, 1 to 2 inches long. Seedling plants are more upright; branches are less pendulous; needles are dark, glossy green up to 4 inches long.

Staking is often necessary to hold up the heavy top while the trunk is gaining strength. African fern pines

African fern pine *(Podocarpus gracilior)* has an open airy habit, making it a good choice for patio or entryway planting.

Yew pine *(Podocarpus macrophyllus)* forms a dense hedge or screen.

Douglas fir (Pseudotsuga menziesii) grows in stately symmetry. A beautiful specimen tree; may be clipped as hedge.

Douglas fir (Pseudotsuga menziesii)

are useful around patios, and entry-ways, and can be used for hedges, espaliers, and even hanging baskets.

Podocarpus macrophyllus
Yew Pine
Zones: 8-10. To 50-60 feet.

A native of Japan and China, yew pine is one of the hardiest species and tolerant of heat and drought. It has a narrow, erect growth habit with short horizontal branches and drooping branchlets. Reaches a height of 8 to 12 feet in 10 years. Makes a good street or lawn tree if thinned and staked. Plant to frame an entryway or as a privacy screen.

Flattened leaves are glossy, bright to dark green, 3 to 4 inches long and 1 4 to 1 2 inch wide with pointed ends. Purplish, 1 2-inch-long fruits are not showy.

Yew pine grows in most soils but does best in a moist loam. Chlorosis may develop in alkaline or heavy, wet soils. In cool areas, it grows best in full sun or light shade. Grow in shade and protect from wind in hot climates. Usually pest-free.

Prunus
Prunus
Zones: 7-10. To 5-45 feet.

Several species in this genus are evergreens that can be trained as trees. However, they are primarily used as shrubs. You will find complete descriptions of the top-rated species in *Top-Rated Evergreen Shrubs*, another book in this series.

Pseudotsuga menziesii
Douglas Fir
Zones: 4-9. To 50-200 feet.

One of the world's most important timber trees, this symmetrical, cone-shaped species is native from British Columbia to California along the coast, and from British Columbia into Mexico in the interior mountains. Grows at sea level in the cool, humid coastal part of its range, but only in the mountains in the interior and southern part of its range.

Typical form for a tree growing in the open is a tall symmetrical cone shape. Limbs at the top of the tree may angle upward, in the middle are horizontal, and at the base are drooping. Limbs are retained to the ground for many years but eventually die, revealing thick, dark brown, deeply furrowed bark on old trees. Bark on younger trees may be smooth gray. Very young stems exhibit pitch-filled blisters.

In spring, shiny reddish-brown, sharply pointed buds open, exposing bright green needles that contrast nicely with the dark green, older needles. Soft, 1- to 1-1/2-inch-long needles are densely spaced all around the stems and persist up to 8 years. A three-pointed bract, projecting from each scale of the slender, 3- to 4-inch, light brown cones, immediately identifies the cone as coming from a Douglas fir. Cones mature each season on trees at least 10 years old and over 15 feet tall. Many variants in needle color and growth habit have been named but are not widely grown.

Growth is best on a moist, but well-drained, acid soil in full sunlight. Trees do not grow, or grow poorly, in alkaline or waterlogged soils, or in those with an impervious layer near the surface.

Christmas trees, specimen plants, windbreaks, and hedges are some of the landscape uses of Douglas fir. Young trees can be sheared for hedge use or to produce a dense Christmas tree. This should be done before new growth has hardened. There is no sprouting if a cut is made into old wood.

Pyrus kawakamii
Evergreen Pear
Zones: 9-10. To 30 feet.

Evergreen pears are prized for their heavy display of flowers in the spring and their glossy foliage. However, in the landscape they can serve a multiple function. A complete description of this species is in *Top-Rated Flowering Trees*, another book in this series.

Schinus

Pepper Tree

Though native to South America, one species, *Schinus molle*, from Peru is so widely planted in California it is called California pepper tree.

Trees are not related to the spice pepper, but the dry fruits resemble peppercorns. The colorful winter fruit and the interesting growth habits of these trees make them top landscape plants. Pollen from male trees of both species causes an allergic reaction in some people.

Schinus molle
California Pepper Tree
Zones: 9-10. To 15-50 feet.

Wide-spreading, heavy branches, with branchlets that hang gracefully, give a weeping willowlike appearance to this fast-growing tree. A gnarled, knobby trunk with light brown bark adds visual interest. Generally a large, spreading tree that needs plenty of growing room.

Compound leaves are 6 to 12 inches long and have 20 to 60 very narrow, light green leaflets that are 1-1 2 to 2 inches long. Yellowish-white flowers in drooping terminal clusters are not showy. Rose to red, 1 4-inch fruits add color from November to May.

Best growth is in full sun on well-drained soil. Tolerates poor drainage, heat, drought, and low fertility. Young plants should be staked.

Tends to litter, dropping fruit, twigs, and old leaves. Rapidly invasive, shallow roots can lift pavement and clog drains. Aphids can disfigure foliage.

Schinus terebinthifolius
Brazilian Pepper Tree
Zones: 9-10. To 15-30 feet.

This moderate- to fast-growing, dense, rounded tree has spreading, horizontal branches producing an umbrella shape. Width and height are about equal. A good tree for patios or as a street tree.

California pepper tree *(Schinus molle)* is a large spreading tree requiring ample growing space. Airy and graceful specimen or shade tree. Foliage shown below.

Redwood *(Sequoia sempervirens)* is a regal specimen tree; dramatic against a skyline.

Giant sequoia *(Sequoiadendron giganteum)* becomes large and statuesque; use as silhouette or specimen tree.

Shiny, dark green compound leaves are 6 to 8 inches long and usually have 7 broad leaflets 1 inch long. Whitish flowers in terminal clusters appear in late summer and are followed by showy, bright red to dull rose-red, 1/8-inch fruits that look colorful from December to March.

Brazilian pepper grows in any well-drained soil in full sun and tolerates dryness. Branches should be thinned and long ones headed back in windy areas. Surface roots form unless watered deeply and infrequently. Choose a tree with fruit on it, since fruit quantity is variable on seed-propagated plants.

Sequoia sempervirens

Redwood, Coast Redwood

Zones: 7-10. To 90-100 feet.

The tallest trees on the North American continent, some reaching 368 feet in height, are members of this species. A redwood will probably reach 70 to 90 feet tall with a spread of 14 to 30 feet in large gardens, during the planter's lifetime.

The coast redwood is an upright, rapid-growing tree with a narrow conical or pyramidal shape when young. Initially branches grow straight out from the trunk, becoming more horizontal and spreading on older trees. Branchlets, covered with either scalelike or flat needle-like leaves, have a tendency to be drooping. Tree trunks have red-brown fibrous bark, are straight, and become massive as the tree grows older.

This geologically ancient tree formerly grew over large areas of the Northern Hemisphere. Today, natural stands of redwoods are found only in the fog belt of northern California and Oregon. Because these rapid-growing trees are so attractive and become so statuesque, many attempts have been made to grow them in other areas. However, coast redwoods rarely reach their prime outside of areas with frequent coastal fog.

Plant in groves, screens, as skyline trees, or as a specimen tree. Can also be clipped as a hedge. Surface roots can be a problem in lawns. Because the coast redwood is so long-lived, it should be planted to remain. Some old trees in the original forest are 2,000 to 3,000 years old.

Foliage color varies from light to dark green in seedlings and can be dense or sparse. 'Aptos Blue' has dense blue-green foliage; 'Santa Cruz' has light green foliage; 'Soquel' has light-textured blue-green foliage; 'Los Altos' has deep green foliage.

Sequoiadendron giganteum

Giant Sequoia, Bigtree

Zones: 6-10. To 90-100 feet.

This species includes the world's largest trees in volume and weight. Trunk diameters have reached up to 37 feet. These massive trees grow at a moderate rate, and after centuries may be 325 feet tall.

Giant sequoia is an isolated remnant of geologically ancient trees left over from the age of the dinosaurs. Today's natural range is a narrow belt 260 miles long, on the west slopes of the Sierra Nevadas. Even in this area the trees grow only in scattered groves.

Young trees are narrowly pyramidal with dense blue-green foliage. Leaves are awl-shaped or scalelike and very different from the coast redwood. Young trees hold their branches. As the tree ages, lower branches are lost, exposing the lower trunk's attractive reddish-brown bark. On ancient trees, bark may be 20 inches, or more, thick. Slower-growing than the coast redwood, it may possibly live longer.

Plant in deep, slightly acid soil with good drainage and aeration, in full sunlight. Should be watered deeply but infrequently once established.

Bigtree is easier to grow than the coast redwood but does not have as many landscape uses. Plant in large open areas as a specimen or silhouette tree, or as a conversation piece. Not suitable for small gardens since it develops too wide a spread. If planted in a lawn, roots may surface and cause problems. Trees planted in Central States and the Northeast are usually killed during severe winters. One tree, 70 feet tall, has been reported growing in Bristol, Connecticut.

Taxus
Yew

This genus contains 8 species of evergreen trees and shrubs native to the Northern Hemisphere. Yews are slow-growing, dense-foliaged evergreens that fill many landscape uses. They come in all shapes and sizes, and are commonly grown as trees or shrubs for foundation plantings, hedges, and as shrubby ornamentals. Planted as screens, they can ensure privacy or hide unpleasant features in the landscape. Tall yews planted behind flowering trees provide landscape contrast.

The use of yews as ornamental plants dates back to Roman times when they were used in formal hedges and topiary work.

Inconspicuous male and female flowers are borne on separate plants. Soft red berries add interest to female plants for the short time they are ripe.

Yews will grow on most types of soil. They will not tolerate poor drainage or water standing around their roots. Excessively windy sites can be damaging to most yews. Sunlight or shade is acceptable.

Most yews root easily from cuttings. Easy to propagate and grow, they are readily available from nurseries. More than one form of plant can often be propagated from the mother plant. Botanists use the term *cultivarient* to indicate a plant that is a different form produced by taking cuttings from different parts of the stock plant. Leader cuttings will produce plants that develop a leader. Side cuttings from

English yew *(Taxus baccata)* is slow growing and has dark green foliage and attractive bark. Foliage shown below.

47

Japanese yew *(Taxus cuspidata)* can be pruned to reveal its framework of branches.

Eastern arborvitae *(Thuja occidentalis)* has bright yellow-green foliage. Used for windbreaks, hedges, and screens.

the ends of branches produce spreading plants that keep growing like a branch.

Yews can withstand heavy pruning or shearing, often necessary to keep a plant symmetrical or within bounds.

Yews should not be planted where livestock could graze on them because all parts of the plant contain the alkaloid taxine. Leaves and seeds are poisonous. Withered leaves or clippings have killed cattle and horses that browsed on them. However, deer browse on yews with no apparent ill effects.

Growing yews to tree size cannot be hurried, but site and cultural practices do have an effect. Plants in the open in full sunlight will grow 3 to 4 times as fast as those in shade. Heavy pruning slows growth. Yews on fertile, moist, well-drained soils grow faster. Do not plant yews where deicing salts can be a problem.

Taxus baccata
English Yew
Zones: 6-9. To 40-60 feet.

This native of Europe, North Africa, and western Asia forms a densely branched, slow-growing, broad, rounded tree. Large trees with trunks up to 10 feet in diameter and heights to 95 feet have been measured in England. Yews with such huge diameters are probably over 1,000 years old, but some trees known to be only 100 years old are 90 feet tall.

Yews in tree form have not been widely grown in the United States. Most emphasis has been on the use of the many shrublike cultivars. However, it is well worth the effort to develop trees as specimens, lining long driveways on large properties, and as screens or tall hedges. They are excellent in the landscape. Attractive dark green foliage, contrasting with the reddish-brown scaly bark, presents a most unusual combination.

The historical background of this yew makes it a conversation piece.

The wood was used in medieval times to make the famous longbow of the English archers. Tradition has Robin Hood's band using it to make their bows.

Taxus cuspidata
Japanese Yew
Zones: 5-9. To 45-65 feet.

There is some variation in the form of Japanese yew. Crowns may be erect or flattened and branches may be upright or spreading. In Japan trees up to 65 feet tall with trunk diameters to 28 inches have been reported. A 50-year-old tree near Wooster, Ohio is 30 feet tall and 15 inches in trunk diameter.

Twigs are slender with dull green foliage marked on the undersides with yellow bands. Bark is reddish to dark brown and scaly on the trunk and larger branches. It often falls in long strips from older trees.

The form 'Capitata' is usually grown from seed and can be controlled by pruning or be allowed to develop in its natural tree form. It makes an ideal specimen or formal accent tree. Plants propagated from branch cuttings are spreading and, although often sold as Japanese yew, are usually listed as the cultivar 'Expansa'.

Thuja
Arborvitae

There are 6 species in this genus of small to medium-sized trees native to North America and eastern Asia. Usually dense pyramidal trees with varied foliage color. Crowns of older trees can become thin. Juvenile leaves are needlelike. Mature foliage is scalelike. Used extensively in landscape plantings because of their slow, compact growth.

Best growth is made in full sunlight, although light shade is acceptable and preferred in very hot climates. Dense or heavy shade produces leggy plants with loose open foliage. Arborvitae do best on fertile, moist but well-drained soils.

Pruning should be done in the spring before new growth begins.

Arborvitae are commonly used in foundation plantings, as windbreaks, tall hedges or screens, and as accent plants. Many dwarf cultivars have been developed.

Thuja occidentalis
Eastern Arborvitae, White Cedar, American Arborvitae
Zones: 3-9. To 40-60 feet.

This dense, broad, pyramidal tree has short upright branches that are held to the base of the tree. Foliage is yellow-green, becoming more yellowish in cold winters. Usually has a single trunk, but multiple stems can develop. Heavy snow can bend or break branches and stems. In areas where heavy snows are expected this problem can be largely eliminated by wrapping the plants in late fall with heavy twine. This holds crowns tight. Single-stemmed forms and cultivars are less damaged by heavy snows than those with multiple stems. Do not plant where deicing salts can be a problem.

This species grows on wet or swampy sites in its natural stands. However, being shallow-rooted on such sites, it is subject to up-rooting by heavy winds. In well-drained locations it becomes more firmly rooted and the problem is not serious.

More than 100 cultivars have been developed. Some small trees are: 'Lutea' with golden foliage, around since 1873; 'Nigra' with dark green foliage; 'Techny' with dark green foliage that holds its color all winter; and 'Pyramidalis', a narrow columnar form, with bright green, soft-textured foliage.

Thuja plicata
Giant Arborvitae, Western Red Cedar
Zones: 6-9. To 50-70 feet.

These narrow pyramidal trees frequently develop several leaders

Giant arborvitae *(Thuja plicata)* has dense, delicately textured foliage, adding visual interest in the garden.

Arborvitae *(Thuja sp.)* are widely adapted slow-growing, compact trees used in a variety of forms in the landscape.

Hemlock trees *(Tsuga sp.)* add skyline interest while making stately specimen trees. Can be trimmed for hedging.

Canadian hemlock *(Tsuga canadensis)* has graceful drooping branchlets. Forms an attractive hedge with little pruning.

when grown as ornamentals. Possibly a better ornamental than *T. occidentalis* because of its darker green foliage and graceful appearance. Will grow in Zone 5 if protected from wind. In timber stands, western red cedar may be 200 feet tall.

Tsuga
Hemlock

Hemlocks are large, graceful trees with fine-textured needles and a nodding leader. They grow in sun or shade.

All the top-rated species are native to the United States and Canada, growing in areas with acid soil, where the air and soil remain moist and relatively cool all year. Root systems are shallow so hemlocks should not be used in exposed areas.

Hemlocks are normally very large forest trees and unless controlled by pruning easily outgrow the typical home landscape. However, unlike most conifers, sprouts will develop when trees are trimmed heavily. They naturally tend to produce multiple leaders. If you desire an ideal specimen form, young trees will require pruning of side leaders to maintain a single central leader. Excellent as trimmed hedges, screens, specimen trees, and windbreaks.

Red spider mites are the principle pest of all species and are troublesome on dry sites.

Tsuga canadensis
Canadian Hemlock
Zones: 5-9. To 60-90 feet.

Dense, broad, pyramidal trees with horizontal branches and drooping outer branchlets, Canadian hemlock is native from Nova Scotia to Wisconsin and south along the Appalachian Mountains to Georgia. Grows at a moderate rate, becoming 30 feet tall in 20 years. Dark, lustrous green needles arranged in two rows on the twigs are 1/2 to 3/4 inch long with two broad white bands underneath. Small, brown cones are 1/2 to 3/4 inch long.

Over 50 varieties with different growth habits and foliage colors have been named. Most are dwarf forms. Weeping forms make graceful small trees.

Tsuga caroliniana
Carolina Hemlock
Zones: 5-7. To 40-70 feet.

A slimmer, shorter, less symmetrical tree than the Canadian hemlock, Carolina hemlock has sparser needles that are grass-green, 3/4 inch long, and are arranged all around the stem instead of in opposite rows. This whorled needle arrangement gives Carolina hemlock a much softer landscape texture. Brown cones are 1 to 1-1/2 inches long. More tolerant of air pollution than the Canadian hemlock. Native to the mountains from southwestern Virginia to Georgia.

Tsuga heterophylla
Western Hemlock
Zones: 5-9. To 100-200 feet.

This fast-growing pyramidal tree has horizontal branches with drooping branchlets and a long hanging leader, giving it a resemblance to the deodar cedar. Can be 50 to 65 feet tall in 20 years.

Feathery branches have fine-textured, dark to yellowish-green needles, 1/4 to 3/4 inch long, arranged in two rows. Many small, 1-inch-long, light brown cones hang at the branch tips.

This giant of the hemlock clan grows well only in moist regions from Alaska to northern California and in the mountains of northern Idaho and western Montana. It can be grown in dry areas but will need regular and plentiful watering. Only selections from Idaho or Montana are hardy in Zones 5 to 6.

Xylosma congestum (X. senticosum)

Shiny Xylosma
Zones: 8-10. To 4-30 feet.

One of the most attractive, easy-to-grow plants for foliage and structural effects, shiny xylosma is native to Japan, Korea, and China.

Uses for this plant are varied, depending on the pruning and cultural practices. Can be used as a single- or multistemmed tree, spreading shrub, ground cover (if the upright stems are cut out), espalier on a wall or fence, a tightly trimmed or natural hedge, or grown in containers 18 inches or larger. Also used for barrier and bank stabilization planting along freeways.

When left alone, an open, graceful, wide-spreading shrub 8 to 10 feet tall will develop. The variety 'Compactum' is slower-growing and matures at about half that size.

Leaves are 1-1/2 to 2 inches long with rounded bases and long tapering points. They are a beautiful shiny yellowish green when mature; bronzy-red when new. Many old leaves drop in April when new growth starts.

Inconspicuous yellow flowers bloom August to September. Black fruits are less than 1/4 inch in diameter and ripen November to December. Some plants have thorns.

Xylosma grows on most soils and is heat-tolerant. Several experiments have shown that it also has outstanding drought tolerance. Little water or fertilizer is required to keep the plant alive. Better growth and appearance result with some watering and fertilizing. Grows best in full sun or light shade. Brief exposure to temperatures down to 10°F in midwinter will not kill the plant, but partial or total defoliation will follow.

Spraying is sometimes necessary to control red spider mites and scale. Leaf yellowing, chlorosis, may be a problem. Use iron sulfate or iron chelates to correct.

Shiny xylosma *(Xylosma congestum)* is a multi-use plant that can be used as a accent tree. Leaves, shown below, are bronzy-red as new growth, turning glossy green.

Caring for Evergreen Trees

Evergreen trees are an investment for the future. Be sure to protect your investment by selecting trees carefully and by keeping them in good condition until planted. If you plant with care and follow recommended procedures, your trees will reward you by prospering. Correct soil preparation and planting techniques help assure successful growth of a healthy young tree.

PREPLANTING CARE

Evergreen trees are sold in two forms: balled-and-burlapped and in containers.

Balled-and-burlapped: These trees, which are best planted in spring or fall, are dug from the field where they grow and the ball of roots and soil is wrapped for shipping. Before planting, keep the foliage moist and water the rootball frequently and slowly from the top. Keep the tree shaded and out of the wind, and plant as soon as possible.

When handling balled-and-burlapped trees, be careful to lift them from the bottom—do not use the trunk as a handle. If the plant seems top-heavy, keep it from falling over by lightly securing the trunk to a fence or wedging the rootball between two heavy objects until you're ready to plant.

Container: Many nursery plants are container-grown, that is they are sold in the pot or container in which the plant was propagated. Available throughout the growing season, they are convenient for the home gardener since they don't have to be planted right away and they adjust quickly to transplanting.

Containers are usually plastic or metal. Most nursery personnel will offer to cut the sides of metal cans

Dwarf Hinoki false cypress *(Chamaecyparis obtusa* 'Nana Gracilis')

Scarlet-flowering gum *(Eucalyptus ficifolia)*

for you. This makes planting easier, but is recommended *only if you plan to plant the same day.* Once cans are cut the rootball dries out quickly.

Many containers are made of dark-colored materials which, when exposed to full sun, can rapidly heat up to root-damaging levels. Shade the container with a board, mounded soil, or low wall.

Container-grown plants have been grown in a special soil mix. To make it as easy as possible for these trees to adjust to the soil conditions found in your garden, you should pay careful attention to soil preparation when planting. By amending your yard's soil with the addition of organic material, you can create a growing medium that will provide a transition between the lightweight soil mix used for container growing, and the heavier soil typical of most gardens.

Pinching or cutting off up to two thirds the length of the candles (new growth) on pine trees promotes denser growth.

53

Soil

Proper amounts of water, air, and nutrients are essential for root growth. Soil composition determines how much of these is available for a plant's use, so check your soil type before planting.

Clay soils are composed of small mineral particles that cling tightly to moisture and nutrients, leaving little room for air. A handful of heavy clay soil feels sticky and squeezes through your fingers in ribbons. Overwatering heavy clay soil is a potential problem. Though the surface appears dry, the root area may be saturated with water—and constant saturation and poor aeration can damage roots.

Sandy soils are composed of relatively large mineral particles. Water and nutrients pass through sandy soils quickly. A handful of moist, sandy soil squeezed into a ball crumbles when released. There is plenty of air for root growth but frequent watering is necessary. Fertilizers must be applied more lightly and more frequently.

Loam soils are intermediate between clay and sandy soils, combining the best characteristics of each. Loam soils retain moisture and nutrients but still allow for good aeration and drainage. A handful of squeezed loam soil forms a loosely packed ball.

DRAINAGE

The drainage quality in the area where you are planting should be looked at carefully. While most evergreen trees can adapt to many different soils, few can flourish in an area with constant poor drainage. If drainage is too slow, air is forced from the soil and roots drown. Check drainage before planting by filling a hole with water and letting it drain. Refill the hole with water and time how long it takes to drain. Water should drain at about one-quarter inch per hour. If it drains more slowly than that, you have two choices: Plant in raised beds or mounds, or bore through the impervious soil with a post-hole digger until the water drains at an acceptable rate. Then fill the bored hole with soil that has been amended to drain faster.

Planting

WHEN TO PLANT

The best time to plant is in the fall, when temperatures are moderate and soil is relatively warm, encouraging root growth. If you live where soil freezes, plant in early fall and mulch after planting. The mulch will moderate temperatures, preventing the alternate freezing and thawing that damages roots of partially established plants.

Spring is the second best planting time. Again, temperatures are moderate, minimizing stress on plants. Summer planting is usually not recommended. High heat coupled with limited roots is often enough to kill young plants. However, if you give extra attention to watering, summer planting can be successful.

THE PLANTING HOLE

Planting techniques vary depending upon whether you are planting a balled-and-burlapped or a container-grown tree. But for both types, you should start with a hole that is twice the width of the roots and six inches deeper. Pack soil in the bottom of the planting hole firmly, water, and allow to drain.

If you are planting from containers, or if the soil you dug out of the hole is very sandy or heavy clay, amend the soil you dug from the hole. Mix two parts soil with one part organic material such as compost, peat moss, or shredded bark. Use this amended soil as backfill to refill the hole around and under the tree's roots. This 2-to-1 mix provides a transition between the usually lightweight container soil mix and heavier garden soil.

Do not mix fertilizer in the hole or with backfill soil. Young roots can be damaged by direct contact with fertilizer. Sprinkle fertilizer on top of the soil and around the plant, then water in.

HOW TO PLANT

Balled-and-burlapped planting: Be careful when moving a balled tree. Use both hands under the rootball or, if the tree is very heavy, get a friend to help you carry it on a tarp or a piece of canvas. Set the rootball on a mound of backfill soil so that it is slightly higher than original nursery soil level. (As planting hole soil compacts, the plant will eventually settle at the original soil level.) Add soil to cover the bottom third of the rootball, cut the twine, and lay back the burlap. Do not remove the burlap; it will eventually rot away. Add more soil, firming it as you do.

Some rootballs need support. If there is any possibility of the entire plant, rootball and all, falling after planting is complete, give it support by driving three short stakes into undisturbed soil, attaching them with twine to the trunk just above soil level.

Most larger balled-and-burlapped trees will need trunks staked for support. Use two stakes, one on each side of the tree, to support trunks. Drive the stakes into the bottom of the planting hole but not through the rootball.

Use strips of cloth, plastic tree tape, or twine enclosed by a section of garden hose to attach the trunk to the stakes. A tree will become stronger and support itself sooner if allowed to sway somewhat with the wind. Attach trunk support stakes no higher than necessary and remove them as soon as possible. Be sure to check ties often to ensure they do not damage the bark.

Once the hole is filled and packed and the tree is staked, form a water basin the size of the transplanted rootball, then flood it several times to soak the soil thoroughly.

Container-grown planting: The planting process for container plants is essentially the same as that used with balled-and-burlapped plants. However, the roots of container plants need extra attention. Once you have removed the can, examine the roots. If they're crowded or coiled on the surface,

Soil

Clay soil has smooth texture and retains moisture.

Sandy soil is gritty, loose, and fast-draining.

Loam soil combines the best features of clay and sandy soils.

Planting

1. Mix organic amendment into garden soil to make backfill mix.

2. Add backfill to planting hole to a depth of about 8 inches.

3. Add water to planting hole to moisten and settle backfill.

4. Loosen roots that the container has forced to coil or circle, and set rootball in planting hole.

5. Position plant so most attractive side is most frequently viewed. Add backfill, firming with your hands.

6. Be sure the original rootball receives ample water the first year after planting.

loosen them with a stick or knife and head them away from the trunk. Cut off any badly damaged roots.

Many larger balled-and-burlapped and container-grown trees will need 1 or 2 tall stakes for trunk support. Drive stakes as close as possible to the rootball. Strips of cloth, plastic tree tape, or twine enclosed by a section of garden hose all serve well to attach the trunk to the stakes.

A tree will become stronger and support itself sooner if allowed to sway somewhat with the wind. Attach trunk support stakes no higher than necessary and remove stakes as soon as possible.

Watering

It is very important to keep newly planted evergreen trees well-watered the first season. Be sure the rootball is thoroughly soaked with each watering.

There are a number of ways to water efficiently: basins, furrows (parallel trenches on each side of the tree), sprinklers, soaker hoses, and drip systems. When watering, try to allow no run-off and confine water to inside the tree's drip line (the area on the ground beneath the outer leaves of a plant), and apply water uniformly. By far the most effective way to water, especially when you are trying to establish new plants, is some form of drip irrigation.

Mulching

A mulch is a layer of material applied on top of soil to cover and protect it. It is an effective way to conserve moisture and it cools soil, an important consideration during hot summers. Mulches help prevent weeds and soil compaction, and they give a planting a finished appearance.

Mulches can be organic, such as compost, sawdust, bark, wood chips, or straw, or they can be inorganic, such as plastic or stone.

Fertilizing

Nitrogen is the only element most evergreen trees require from a fertilizer. Young trees may grow more rapidly following nitrogen fertilization, but mature trees usually need little or no fertilization as long as they have good leaf color and are growing well.

Let the tree's condition be your guide to fertilizing. Evergreen trees deficient in nitrogen have light yellow foliage and grow slowly. The yellowing is first evident predominately on older leaves but should not be confused with natural yearly leaf loss. Needlessly stimulating growth may result in more harm than good. Succulent growth caused by overfertilization is more attractive to insects and disease pests.

Fertilizer recommendations are usually made in pounds of actual nitrogen. Infertile soils may require annual applications of about 1 to 1-1/2 pounds of nitrogen per mature tree per year. New plants that show need of nitrogen are adequately served by applying at a rate of 3 to 6 ounces of actual nitrogen per 100 square feet. Keep fertilizers away from the trunk and apply in a radius of 1-1/4 times the radius of the tree's canopy.

To determine how much fertilizer to apply, divide the amount of nitrogen you need by the first number of the fertilizer analysis on the bag (the first number is the number for nitrogen). For example, if you want 1 pound of actual nitrogen and your fertilizer analysis is 20-0-0, divide 1 by 20% (.20). You will need 5 pounds of 20-0-0 to equal 1 pound of actual nitrogen.

Most evergreen trees grow best when soil pH (the measure of acid-alkaline balance) is slightly acid. Soils that are excessively acid or alkaline prevent the tree's efficient use of soil nutrients. Where soil is naturally acid (east of the Mississippi River and in the Northwest) add ground dolomitic limestone to raise the pH. Where soil is naturally alkaline, lower the pH with agricultural sulfur. A soil test is the only way to determine the pH of your garden soil. Soil testing kits are available in most garden centers, or contact your local agricultural extension agent or a private soil testing laboratory.

Pruning

PRUNING BROAD-LEAVED EVERGREENS

Before pruning your newly planted tree, consider again how you're going to use it in your landscape and its particular growth habits. The height of the first permanent branch depends on what you want the tree to do. Is it going to screen an unwanted view? Does there need to be room for children to play beneath it? The position of a branch on the trunk remains the same throughout the life of a tree. As it increases in diameter, the branch gets somewhat closer to the ground.

As you examine your young tree, identify the leader, or main stem, which will be the trunk of your tree. Unless you prefer a multistemmed type, you need to cut out any competing leaders. Now select two or four scaffold (primary) branches above the height that will give you the amount of room you want beneath the tree. Try to choose wide-angled scaffold branches. Branches angled 45° to 90° in relation to the trunk are much stronger than narrow-angled branches. Cut the scaffold branches back to an outward-facing bud so they are not as tall as the leader.

Cut back any branches below the scaffold branches to a single bud. A small amount of foliage along the main trunk will help strengthen it and prevents sunburn. Continue to keep these short lateral branches pruned back so small bunches of foliage are retained. Remove these completely when the tree matures.

The first 2 to 3 years after planting are the most important in developing the permanent framework of your tree. The second year's pruning is often critical in the life of a young tree. It is likely a well cared for young tree has produced heavy shoots and foliage that the leader is not yet able to support. If not pruned properly, some branches may even break off. As you remove this weight, keep in mind the kind of tree shape you want to encourage. For an open shape, leave the terminal (end)

Watering

A soaker hose applies water efficiently at a rate soil can absorb, directly over rootball.

A basin of firmed soil directs water to roots—however periodic repair is required.

Drip watering systems conserve water by applying it only where necessary.

Mulching

Bark mulch is available in many sizes. It conserves moisture and gives plantings a finished appearance.

Rock mulch does not wash away and lasts indefinitely, but does not add humus to soil.

Irregular particles of low-cost shredded bark bind together to form a mulch that will hold well on slopes.

Fertilizing

Granular fertilizer applied on surface can promote good tree growth but often is consumed primarily by lawn.

Subsurface injector delivers water and nutrients directly to root zone.

Spray leaves with foliar fertilizer for fastest results.

shoot on the scaffold branches and shorten or remove all side shoots. For a compact shape, cut the terminals back to a side shoot on each branch. This will help the branches grow thicker and more horizontal.

Thinning: Thinning becomes necessary when the interior growth of a tree begins to get too dense and casts too heavy a shade. Thinning gives a tree a more open structure. To thin a tree, remove large and small branches at their points of origin or cut them back to main branches. After thinning, the new growth follows the tree's natural branching pattern and tends to be evenly distributed throughout the crown.

Heading back: In many ways the opposite of thinning, heading back is done to encourage denser, more compact growth. Hedges and screens are commonly headed back, however it results in less strongly attached branches that are more likely to break.

Head back a tree in early spring by cutting back branch tips several inches to a lateral bud, or to a lateral branch. After heading back, new growth comes from one or several buds near the cut; lower buds don't normally grow. Heading can be a useful technique for young trees, controlling size and promoting dense growth. When mature trees are headed, it is called stubbing. Stubbing is rarely attractive or beneficial to the tree.

PRUNING CONIFERS

Though conifers do not need pruning as often as broad-leaved evergreen trees, they do need it—to remove deadwood, to control size and shape, and to reduce wind resistance. Unlike the broad-leaved plants, most needled trees do not produce latent buds on wood without foliage; if they are cut back to a stub, no new growth will follow. However, yew, arborvitae, hemlock, sequoia, some junipers, and some pines are important exceptions.

Most conifers have a central leader, or main trunk. Unless you are trying to restrict the height of the tree, don't damage the leader. Branches radiate from the leader either at random or in vertical whorls around the trunk. Random-branching conifers, which have an informal shape—arborvitae, sequoia, yew—can be pruned by clipping back branch tips to control size and shape. Whorl-branching species—fir, pine, spruce—which grow in basically symmetrical shapes—will form closer whorls if new growth is cut back to a bud. Be sure to prune these conifers while new growth is immature and flexible.

New growth of pines is produced in long shoots known as "candles". Snapping or cutting off candles by one half to two thirds their length before needles enlarge will encourage denser growth.

When conifers are within about a foot of the mature size you want, cut all new growth so that only about an inch of it remains; this will produce small lateral branches that will make the tree more dense but not increase its size.

Columnar-shaped conifers can be shaped by cutting upright branches back to short, spreading laterals, or in larger specimens, heading back widely spreading branches just inside the foliage line. Many evergreens, such as hemlock and spruce, have branches all the way to the ground. For the most handsome shape, do not remove these low branches.

HEDGES

Hedges are shaped by heading back frequently. Shearing with two-handed hedge clippers promotes a dense outer layer of foliage, but leaves the inside of the shrub bare. Shearing produces a hedge that has a neat, formal appearance. For a more natural and informal-looking hedge, prune with a one-handed pruning tool. Reach inside the shrub and cut out selected long branches, maintaining the natural shape of the plant. This procedure thins the interior of the plant and promotes thick foliage. Shorten tips of remaining branches.

Problems and Solutions

Some evergreen trees are subject to attack by insect pests such as aphids, including cooly spruce gall aphids and woolly aphids, scale, spider mites, thrips, caterpillars, and mealybugs. Cedar-apple rust, Texas (or cotton) root rot, and white pine blister rust are diseases that may infect certain species of evergreen trees. To help you avoid inviting these garden problems to your home, general information on specific pests and diseases is included in the plant listings where they apply. You will also find a column in the care charts on pages 60 to 62 that tells you whether or not an evergreen tree is considered to be pest-resistant.

Insect pests and diseases can be controlled chemically, physically, or biologically. The trend in recent years has been away from chemical spraying in favor of physical controls—such as hosing pests off—and biological controls—encouraging useful insects such as ladybugs and lacewings to stay in the garden. Effective controls vary, depending on season, region, and the type of weather when treatment is administered.

Following good maintenance procedures in your garden and being observant can minimize problems. Early detection of insect pests or diseases and prompt treatment can help keep the problem from becoming serious in most cases.

If you spot symptoms of disease or pest infestation, such as brown or spotted leaves, dead branches, unusual growths or cracked oozing bark, cut off a small portion of the infected plant and take it to your local garden center. Your nurseryman can identify the problem and recommend the most effective treatment program.

Another good source of information about plant pests and diseases is your County Agricultural or Extension Agent. To locate that office, look in your phone book under the name of your county for the Cooperative Extension Service listing.

Pruning

Control size and shape of arborvitae, hemlock, false cypress, yew, juniper and sequoia by clipping back branch tips lightly, anytime.

For denser growth of fir and spruce, prune new growth on lateral branches back half-way, cutting back to a pair of buds or other laterals.

Snap or cut back "candles" on pines by one half to two thirds their length before needles enlarge, to promote denser growth.

Thin broad-leaved evergreens to direct growth and establish desired shape: (left) Thinning cuts made; (right) Resulting growth.

Head to increase the number of new shoots and stiffen branches of broad-leaved evergreens: (left) Heading cuts made; (right) Resulting growth.

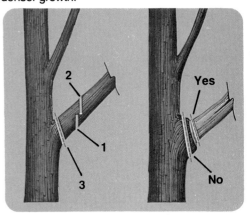

To remove heavy limb (left): 1) Undercut, 2) Cut through limb, 3) Remove stub. To remove dead stub (right): Cut flush with healthy growth, not trunk.

Problems and Solutions

Your nurseryman can give excellent advice and suggest solutions to your garden problems.

Pines, spruce, hemlock, fir, and some cedars are often infested by pine needle scale. Control these insect pests by applying dormant oil sprays.

If chemical spraying for insect control is necessary, follow directions on insecticide label carefully.

Planting and Care of Evergreen Trees

This chart presents in simplified form basic information about the planting requirements and follow-up care for each of the evergreen trees discussed in this book. Use it as a quick reference when determining what conditions and care a particular evergreen tree needs to grow successfully. More detailed information on planting and care of particular plants is contained in the encyclopedia listings.

PLANT NAME	Exposure			Water			Soil					Fertilizer			Pruning			Pest Resistant
	Sun	Partial Shade	Shade	Plenty	Regular	Drought Tolerant	Acid	Alkaline	Well-drained	Fertile	Infertile	Heavy	Regular	Light	Heading	Thinning	Season	
Abies concolor	■				■	■	■	■	■	■			■	■	■	■[8]	spring	yes
Abies nordmanniana	■				■		■	■	■	■			■	■	■	■[8]	spring	yes
Arbutus menziesii	■	■		■	■	■[1]	■		■		■			■		■	late winter	yes
Arbutus unedo	■	■	■[2]	■	■	■	■	■	■	■	■		■	■		■	anytime	yes
Cedrus atlantica	■				■	■	■	■	■	■				■		■[8]	spring	yes
Cedrus deodara	■				■	■	■	■	■	■				■		■[8]	spring	yes
Cedrus libani	■				■	■	■	■	■	■				■			spring	yes
Ceratonia siliqua	■				■	■		■	■	■	■			■	■[10]	■	spring	yes
Chamaecyparis lawsoniana	■	■[3]			■		■		■	■			■		■[10]	■	early spring	yes
Chamaecyparis obtusa	■				■		■	■	■	■			■		■[10]	■	early spring	yes
Chamaecyparis pisifera	■				■		■		■	■			■		■[10]	■	early spring	yes
Cinnamomum camphora	■				■	■	■	■	■	■			■	■	■[10]	■	anytime	yes
x Cupressocyparis leylandii	■				■		■	■	■	■			■	■	■[10]	■	late spring	yes
Cupressus arizonica	■				■	■		■	■	■	■		■	■	■[10]	■	late spring	yes
Cupressus macrocarpa	■				■		■	■	■		■		■	■	■[10]	■	late spring	no
Cupressus sempervirens	■				■	■	■	■	■	■	■		■	■	■[10]		late spring	no
Eucalyptus sp.	■				■	■	■	■	■	■	■		■	■	■	■	early spring	yes
Feijoa sellowiana	■	■			■	■	■	■	■	■					■[10]	■	late spring	yes
Ficus benjamina	■	■	■	■	■		■		■	■		■	■		■[10]	■	early spring	yes

[1] — Drought tolerant once established; [2] — Needs shade in desert; [3] — Partial shade only in southern areas; [4] — Partial shade in hot summer areas; [5] — Tolerates plenty of water; [6] — Partial shade in inland desert; [7] — Moderate; [8] — Pinch tips; [9] — Pinch candles; [10] — Takes shearing.

PLANT NAME	Exposure			Water			Soil					Fertilizer			Pruning			Pest Resistant
	Sun	Partial Shade	Shade	Plenty	Regular	Drought Tolerant	Acid	Alkaline	Well-drained	Fertile	Infertile	Heavy	Regular	Light	Heading	Thinning	Season	
Ficus elastica	■	■	■	■	■		■		■	■		■	■			■	early spring	yes
Ficus lyrata	■	■		■			■		■	■		■	■			■	early spring	yes
Ficus retusa	■	■		■	■		■	■	■	■		■	■		■[10]	■	early spring	no
Ficus rubiginosa	■	■			■	■	■	■	■	■			■			■	early spring	yes
Fraxinus uhdei	■				■	■		■	■	■	■		■	■		■	winter or early spring	yes
Hymenosporum flavum	■	■			■	■	■		■	■		■	■			■	early spring	yes
Ilex x altaclarensis 'Wilsonii'	■	■	■	■	■	■[1]	■	■	■	■			■	■	■[10]	■	early spring	yes
Ilex aquifolium	■	■[2]		■	■	■[1]	■		■				■		■	■	early spring	no
Ilex opaca	■				■		■			■					■[10]	■	early spring	yes
Juniperus scopulorum	■				■	■		■	■	■	■	■	■	■	■[10]	■	early spring	yes
Juniperus virginiana	■			■	■	■	■	■	■	■	■	■	■	■	■[10]	■	early spring	yes
Laurus nobilis	■	■[4]			■		■	■	■	■			■		■[10]	■	early spring	no
Ligustrum japonicum	■	■			■	■	■	■	■	■		■	■	■	■[10]	■	late winter	yes
Ligustrum lucidum	■	■			■	■	■	■	■	■		■	■	■	■[10]	■	late winter	yes
Magnolia grandiflora	■			■[5]	■		■		■	■		■	■			■	late summer	yes
Magnolia virginiana	■				■	■	■		■	■		■	■			■	late summer	yes
Olea europaea	■				■	■	■	■	■	■	■	■	■	■	■	■	early spring	yes
Picea abies	■			■	■		■	■	■	■		■	■	■	■[8]	■	spring	no
Picea glauca	■				■		■	■	■	■		■	■	■	■[8]	■	spring	yes
Picea omorika	■				■	■	■	■	■	■		■	■	■	■[8]	■	spring	yes
Picea pungens	■				■	■	■	■	■	■		■	■	■	■[8]	■	spring	no
Pinus aristata	■				■	■	■	■	■	■		■	■	■	■[9]	■	spring	yes
Pinus bungeana	■				■	■	■	■	■	■		■	■	■	■[9]	■	spring	yes
Pinus canariensis	■				■	■	■	■	■	■		■	■	■	■[9]	■	spring	yes

[1] — Drought tolerant once established; [2] — Needs shade in desert; [3] — Partial shade only in southern areas; [4] — Partial shade in hot summer areas; [5] — Tolerates plenty of water; [6] — Partial shade in inland desert; [7] — Moderate; [8] — Pinch tips; [9] — Pinch candles; [10] — Takes shearing.

Plant Name	Exposure			Water			Soil					Fertilizer			Pruning			Pest Resistant
	Sun	Partial Shade	Shade	Plenty	Regular	Drought Tolerant	Acid	Alkaline	Well-drained	Fertile	Infertile	Heavy	Regular	Light	Heading	Thinning	Season	
Pinus contorta	■	■[6]			■	■	■		■	■	■		■	■	■[9]	■	spring	yes
Pinus densiflora	■				■	■	■	■	■	■	■		■	■	■[9]	■	spring	yes
Pinus halepensis	■					■		■			■			■	■[9]	■	spring	yes
Pinus nigra	■				■	■				■	■			■	■[9]	■	spring	yes
Pinus patula	■				■	■	■	■	■	■			■	■	■[9]	■	spring	yes
Pinus pinaster	■				■	■	■	■	■		■			■	■[9]	■	spring	yes
Pinus pinea	■				■	■	■	■	■	■	■		■	■	■[9]	■	spring	yes
Pinus strobus	■				■		■	■	■	■	■		■	■	■[9]	■	spring	no
Pinus sylvestris	■				■	■	■	■	■	■	■		■	■	■[9]	■	spring	yes
Pinus thunbergiana	■				■	■	■	■	■	■	■	■	■	■	■[9]	■	spring	yes
Podocarpus gracilior	■	■	■[2]	■	■		■	■	■	■			■		■[10]	■	early spring	yes
Podocarpus macrophyllus	■	■	■[2]	■	■		■	■	■	■			■		■[10]	■	early spring	yes
Pseudotsuga menziesii	■	■		■	■		■		■	■	■	■	■		■[10]	■	early spring	yes
Schinus molle	■				■	■	■	■	■	■	■		■	■	■	■	early spring	yes
Schinus terebinthifolius	■				■	■	■	■	■	■	■		■	■	■	■	early spring	yes
Sequoia sempervirens	■	■		■	■	■[1]	■	■	■	■			■		■[10]		early spring	yes
Sequoiadendron giganteum	■				■	■	■[7]		■	■	■	■	■			■	early spring	yes
Taxus baccata	■	■			■	■[1]	■	■	■	■			■		■[10]		early spring	yes
Taxus cuspidata	■	■			■	■[1]	■	■	■	■			■		■[10]		early spring	yes
Thuja occidentalis	■	■[2]		■	■		■	■	■	■			■	■	■		early spring	no
Thuja plicata	■	■[2]		■	■	■	■	■	■	■			■	■	■		early spring	yes
Tsuga canadensis	■	■[2]		■	■		■		■	■			■	■	■[10]		early spring	no
Tsuga caroliniana	■	■[2]		■	■		■		■	■			■	■	■[10]		early spring	no
Tsuga heterophylla	■	■[2]		■	■		■		■	■			■	■	■[10]		early spring	no
Xylosma congestum	■	■			■	■	■	■	■	■	■		■	■	■[10]	■	early spring	yes

[1] — Drought tolerant once established; [2] — Needs shade in desert; [3] — Partial shade only in southern areas; [4] — Partial shade in hot summer areas; [5] — Tolerates plenty of water; [6] — Partial shade in inland desert; [7] — Moderate; [8] — Pinch tips; [9] — Pinch candles; [10] — Takes shearing.

Name Cross-Reference

A plant can have many common names but has only one proper botanical name. The following list matches common names with their botanical names. The parts of a botanical name are the *genus*, *species*, and *cultivar* (or variety). The genus name signifies the general group to which the plant belongs, and together with the species name describes a particular plant. The cultivar is the name between quotation marks. An "x" between the genus and the species indicates the plant is a hybrid, formed either naturally or by breeders.

Common Name	Botanical Name
Arborvitae, American	*Thuja occidentalis*
Arborvitae, Eastern	*Thuja occidentalis*
Arborvitae, Giant	*Thuja plicata*
Ash, Evergreen	*Fraxinus uhdei*
Ash, Shamel	*Fraxinus uhdei*
Bigtree	*Sequoiadendron giganteum*
Bull Bay	*Magnolia grandiflora*
Bushy Yate	*Eucalyptus lehmannii*
Camphor Tree	*Cinnamomum camphora*
Carob	*Ceratonia siliqua*
Cedar, Atlas	*Cedrus atlantica*
Cedar, Deodar	*Cedrus deodara*
Cedar, Eastern Red	*Juniperus virginiana*
Cedar, Western Red	*Thuja plicata*
Cedar, White	*Thuja occidentalis*
Cedar-of-Lebanon	*Cedrus libani*
Coast Redwood	*Sequoia sempervirens*
Cypress, Arizona	*Cupressus arizonica*
Cypress, False	*Chamaecyparis sp.*
Cypress, Hinoki False	*Chamaecyparis obtusa*
Cypress, Italian	*Cupressus sempervirens*
Cypress, Lawson	*Chamaecyparis lawsoniana*
Cypress, Leyland	*x Cupressocyparis leylandii*
Cypress, Monterey	*Cupressus macrocarpa*
Cypress, Sawara	*Chamaecyparis pisifera*
Douglas Fir	*Pseudotsuga menziesii*
Eucalyptus	*Eucalyptus sp.*
Eucalyptus, Fuchsia	*Eucalyptus forrestiana*
Evergreen Ash	*Fraxinus uhdei*
False Cypress	*Chamaecyparis sp.*
Fern Pine, African	*Podocarpus gracilior*
Fig, Fiddle-Leaf	*Ficus lyrata*
Fig, Indian Laurel	*Ficus retusa*
Fig, Rusty	*Ficus rubiginosa*
Fig, Weeping	*Ficus benjamina*
Fir, Douglas	*Pseudotsuga menziesii*
Fir, Nordmann	*Abies nordmanniana*
Fir, White	*Abies concolor*
Giant Sequoia	*Sequoiadendron giganteum*
Glossy Privet	*Ligustrum lucidum*
Grecian Laurel	*Laurus nobilis*
Guava, Pineapple	*Feijoa sellowiana*
Gum, Cider	*Eucalyptus gunnii*
Gum, Coral	*Eucalyptus torquata*
Gum, Desert	*Eucalyptus rudis*
Gum, Lemon-Scented	*Eucalyptus citriodora*
Gum, Manna	*Eucalyptus viminalis*
Gum, Red	*Eucalyptus camaldulensis*
Gum, Scarlet-Flowering	*Eucalyptus ficifolia*
Gum, Silver-Dollar	*Eucalyptus polyanthemos*
Hemlock, Canadian	*Tsuga canadensis*
Hemlock, Carolina	*Tsuga caroliniana*
Hemlock, Western	*Tsuga heterophylla*
Holly, American	*Ilex opaca*
Holly, Christmas	*Ilex aquifolium*

Common Name	Botanical Name
Holly, English	*Ilex aquifolium*
Holly, Wilson	*Ilex x altaclarensis* 'Wilsonii'
Juniper, Rocky Mountain	*Juniperus scopulorum*
Laurel, Grecian	*Laurus nobilis*
Madrone	*Arbutus menziesii*
Magnolia, Southern	*Magnolia grandiflora*
Magnolia, Sweet Bay	*Magnolia virginiana*
Narrow-Leaved Gimlet	*Eucalyptus spathulata*
Nichol's Willow-Leaved Peppermint	*Eucalyptus nicholii*
Olive	*Olea europaea*
Pepper Tree, Brazilian	*Schinus terebinthifolius*
Pepper Tree, California	*Schinus molle*
Pine, African Fern	*Podocarpus gracilior*
Pine, Aleppo	*Pinus halepensis*
Pine, Austrian Black	*Pinus nigra*
Pine, Bristlecone	*Pinus aristata*
Pine, Canary Island	*Pinus canariensis*
Pine, Cluster	*Pinus pinaster*
Pine, French Turpentine	*Pinus pinaster*
Pine, Italian Stone	*Pinus pinea*
Pine, Japanese Black	*Pinus thunbergiana*
Pine, Japanese Red	*Pinus densiflora*
Pine, Jelecote	*Pinus patula*
Pine, Lacebark	*Pinus bungeana*
Pine, Maritime	*Pinus pinaster*
Pine, Scotch	*Pinus sylvestris*
Pine, Shore	*Pinus contorta*
Pine, White	*Pinus strobus*
Pine, Yew	*Podocarpus macrophyllus*
Pineapple Guava	*Feijoa sellowiana*
Pink Ironbark	*Eucalyptus sideroxylon*
Privet, Glossy	*Ligustrum lucidum*
Privet, Japanese	*Ligustrum japonicum*
Redwood	*Sequoia sempervirens*
Rubber Plant	*Ficus elastica*
St. John's-Bread	*Ceratonia siliqua*
Sequoia, Giant	*Sequoiadendron giganteum*
Shamel Ash	*Fraxinus uhdei*
Shiny Xylosma	*Xylosma congestum*
Silver-Dollar Tree	*Eucalyptus cinerea*
Spruce, Colorado	*Picea pungens*
Spruce, Colorado Blue	*Picea pungens* 'Glauca'
Spruce, Norway	*Picea abies*
Spruce, Serbian	*Picea omorika*
Spruce, White	*Picea glauca*
Strawberry Tree	*Arbutus unedo*
Swamp Mallee	*Eucalyptus spathulata*
Sweet Bay	*Laurus nobilis*, *Magnolia virginiana*
Sweetshade	*Hymenosporum flavum*
Weeping Chinese Banyan	*Ficus benjamina*
Xylosma, Shiny	*Xylosma congestum*
Yate Tree	*Eucalyptus cornuta*
Yew, English	*Taxus baccata*
Yew, Japanese	*Taxus cuspidata*
Yew Pine	*Podocarpus macrophyllus*

Index

Main plant listings indicated by bold numbers.

C   D   E   F